How Do You Spell Ruzevelt?

How Do You Spell Ruzevelt?

A History of Spelling in America Today and Yesterday

M ARSHA E. A CKERMANN

WITH T HOMAS K. B LACK III

ARCHWAY
PUBLISHING

Archway Publishing books may be ordered through booksellers or by contacting:

Archway Publishing
1663 Liberty Drive
Bloomington, IN 47403
www.archwaypublishing.com
1-(888)-242-5904

Because of the dynamic nature of the Internet, any web addresses or
links contained in this book may have changed since publication and
may no longer be valid. The views expressed in this work are solely those
of the author and do not necessarily reflect the views of the publisher,
and the publisher hereby disclaims any responsibility for them.

Any people depicted in stock imagery provided by Thinkstock are models,
and such images are being used for illustrative purposes only.
Certain stock imagery © Thinkstock.

ISBN: 978-1-4808-1092-1 (sc)
ISBN: 978-1-4808-1093-8 (e)

Library of Congress Control Number: 2014915517

Printed in the United States of America.

Archway Publishing rev. date: 9/17/2014

For instance, take the monosyllable Cat. What a brazen forehead you must have when you say to an infant, c, a, t, – spell Cat: that is, three sounds, forming a totally opposite compound...Don't they rather compose the sound see-eh-te, or ceaty? How can a system of education flourish that begins with so monstrous a falsehood?

From *The Caxtons* by
Edward Bulwer Lytton, 1849

Acknowledgements

An ability to spell came to me early, but thinking about spelling has taken much longer. Twenty-two years after I participated in the Scripps National Spelling Bee I finally returned to this most banal, yet mysterious aspect of the English language when I attended the 1985 Bee and wrote an op-ed article for the *Washington Post* titled "The Invasion of the Spelling People." And it took a mere twenty-one years more before I finally found my way into this book. I sorely miss my peerless spelling coach, Lee Metzstein Ackermann, and my brother, John, who cheered me on, way back in 1963. My stepdaughter, Katherine, has become a careful and caring speller and alerted me to a new GPO spelling manual. My husband Thom can spot a typo or outright gaffe at fifty paces and is as much a spelling stickler as I am.

Contents

Introduction

It is June 1963. In Washington, D.C.'s then venerably shabby Mayflower Hotel, thirty boys and thirty-nine girls are competing in the thirty-sixth National Spelling Bee. Contestant #57 is a rather tall eighth-grader, just turned thirteen. She is clutching a "lucky" plastic troll figure and, on the first day of the contest, wears the same blue shirtwaist dress in which she had won the Western New York spelling championship a month earlier. Both her school, Sweet Home Central in Amherst, New York, and her sponsor, the *Buffalo Evening News*, have had trouble spelling her name correctly, but Washington Bureau reporter Robert C. Jensen gets it right in a front page story and photo. She has made it through the first day's ten rounds. Along with the other surviving spellers, she is oblivious to the news that shares front pages across the nation – the assassination of Mississippi civil rights leader Medgar Evers.

This girl, as you have likely surmised, was (and is) I. And no, I was not to become the 1963 national champion. The word I missed – *dilatory* -- was easy enough but unfamiliar. I asked for a synonym. "Delay," they told me. "Deeelay." So I spelled it "delatory." Dinggg! My final ranking was twenty-fifth. My mother, Lee, formerly Liebe, who was born in Berlin speaking German and Yiddish, had coached me through "Words of the Champions," the Sixties version of the official Bee study booklet. She suggested a protest but I demurred. Clearly it was my own fault. On that second day I had ditched my "lucky" dress in favor of a different outfit. Glen Van Slyke III of Knoxville, Tennessee became the champion when he spelled *equipage*.

Spelling Bee Memorabilia

Literature compiled by Bee officials in 1963 showed that at least eighteen finalists had learned their spelling in parochial schools. Only one contestant seemed more "foreign" than I was. He was Karlis Rusa of Indianapolis whose Bee blurb noted that he had been born in a displaced persons camp as his Latvian parents fled the Soviets at the end of World War II. While his parents continued to speak in their native tongue, Karlis mastered English, spoke some German, and was working on French.

Twenty-two years later, I was a guest observer at the Scripps Bee won by Balu Natarajan, the very first of many recent champions born to Indian parents. When he correctly spelled "dilatoriness" in an early round I knew he would go all the way. I did not remember a single one of the words I had spelled correctly during my two days on stage until I found a cache of yellowing articles from the

Buffalo *paper*. Serious spellers almost always recall their flubs, but few remember very many of the words that did not get away.

More than a century before the dawn of modern spelling contests, Americans were already vigorously contesting spelling itself. In 1786, young Noah Webster made a stunning assertion. A Yale College graduate who had seen some action in the American Revolution and then briefly and unhappily taught school, he had recently published a children's spelling book that soon made him a household name. Soon he would offer his countrymen their very own precisely spelled and properly pronounced language. It would be a truly American tongue, liberated from all of the inconsistencies, difficulties, and peculiarities that marred the language of the recently defeated British. His reforms, Webster claimed, would "render the acquisition of the language easy both for natives and foreigners." Furthermore, he said, "All the trouble of learning to spell will be saved."

Could he possibly have been more wrong?

This is a historical investigation into the origins, meaning, and consequences of the United States' way of spelling, from Webster's cocksure prediction to a twenty-first century of spell-checkers, "invented" spelling, texting, and prime time televised spelling bees. It is a story rich in pedants, publishers, and politicians; dreamers, schemers, and reformers.

It also invokes larger themes. Language, in both its spoken and written forms, is fundamentally entwined in national and personal identity. Much was at stake in the world's first large republic as Americans struggled to use an evolving language to meet the challenge of new political, economic, and social arrangements.

The new United States was a hodge-podge of nationalities, races, religions, and occupations. Only a few former colonists could boast European standards of education and refinement. Language debates were ferocious, running the gamut from fawning Anglophilia to patriotic hubris, and seemed to agree only that some version of "proper" language anchored by correct pronunciation and spelling, was essential to the success of the democratic enterprise. Some called

George Washington a dunce, and even Thomas Jefferson, principal author of the Declaration of Independence, was a "whimsical"
and inconsistent speller. College-educated men, then concentrated
mainly in New England and New York, spearheaded, but could not
always dominate arguments over how to cultivate in Americans a
level of "democratic eloquence" suitable for a new society that was
surely poised for greatness.

The era of Benjamin Franklin and Noah Webster where this
story begins, offers lessons in the meaning of Americanism that were
contested in every possible way. The politics of this new era and new
order extended well beyond who could vote and who would rule.
Spelling and spelling education became one of many battlefronts. On
this seminal level of language, Webster and many others experienced
intense anxiety about what the Declaration of Independence had
so recently called the "unalienable right" to Liberty. Was America's
new-minted independence to be a wholesome and constructive force,
or would Liberty emerge as its own "evil twin" of anarchic excess?
Corrupted or careless language, many believed, could prove as dangerous to Young America as venal leaders or ruinous taxes.

Ideology proved to be no barrier to commerce. Many men (and
a few women) of letters saw new and urgent opportunities for influence, and even wealth. As locally printed books began to rival British
imports, pamphlets, newspapers, religious tracts, instructional texts,
and even novels, poetry, and drama, proliferated across the new
nation. Webster was not the only person of his era to see the patriotic
and commercial possibilities of "translating" English into a truly
American language, defined in part by its more republican and
presumably more rational, vigorous, and, perhaps, easier spelling.
Orthography is the Greek-rooted word that means right or correct
spelling, and spelling is but one of many language issues that engage, infuriate, and puzzle all who would use the English language.
Spelling can be distinguished from associated aspects of language
and literacy, including grammar, punctuation, usage, etymology,
oratory, and even penmanship, by its commonplace ubiquity.

Everybody knows what spelling is, even those who do not spell very well. Differences between American and British spelling, although really quite minimal, still provoke disparaging comments on either side of the "pond." Many people, not all of them excellent spellers, consider spelling to be the most elementary of language skills, hardly more challenging (or useful) than chanting the twenty-six letters of the alphabet – or spelling "C-A-T." For many decades, such chanting, soon followed by learning to spell supposedly simple syllables, defined the American child's first language achievement, which might prove to be his or her last. In one of his earliest *New York Times Magazine* language columns, the late "wordmonger" William Safire wrote, "Most of us are proud of two things we ought to be ashamed of: illegible handwriting and poor spelling." He cheerfully added, "The truth is that I have never been good at spelling, which most of my teachers and friends never knew, because they couldn't read my handwriting. But at least I'm not proud of either."

Spelling seems to be simple; after all (some) six-year-olds learn it. And it almost always requires a binary result: a word is spelled either right or wrong. Spelling contests from one-room schoolhouses to today's national Bees would surely disappoint if their outcomes were not orthographically correct. But such contests make sense only because our spelling is in fact immensely complex. Despite a plethora of guides, rules, hints, reverse dictionaries, and now automatic spellcheckers, there is still no reliably intuitive correspondence between how a word sounds when it is spoken and how it looks on the page. English is not a phonetic language even though phonics may help children learn to spell. A great many sounds produced in English do not actually correspond to the customary sound of any of the twenty-six letters in an alphabet that many experts and ordinary users alike have long considered defective. This gap between sound and sense is at once the English language's greatest drawback and its most exciting and challenging attribute.

Consider two common words: *bare* and *bear*. *Bare* has a relatively simple meaning: it exposes your soul, your teeth, or your body.

Bear is a *homonym*. This means that the exact same set of letters in this common word correctly spells a large furry mammal, the act of birthing a baby, or holding up under pressure. But wait: *bare* is a *homophone*. It sounds exactly like *bear* but is spelled differently. So if you plan to write about a bare bear, precise spelling is a must.

Good spellers gleefully enjoy the many opportunities for puns offered by such spelling peculiarities. Others are less enthusiastic.

Doctor Samuel Johnson, who compiled Britain's first dictionary in 1755, admitted that he was nearly overwhelmed by "the boundless chaos of a living speech." Almost a century later, American philosopher Ralph Waldo Emerson called English "the sea which receives tributaries from every region under heaven." Linguists, especially those who oppose phonetic "fixes" for English spelling, have likewise noted that the language that became English over many centuries borrowed voraciously from many other languages (as it does still) and retained the husks and forms of sounds that have shifted in pronunciation or are no longer used at all. The spelling of English is a complex feat that honors that ancient and continuing legacy.

This story starts at the cusp of American colonialism and independence. Chapter 1, "Young America's 'Spelling Blues'" describes how spelling and related language issues played into efforts to define the new nation. Benjamin Franklin, Noah Webster, Horace Mann, and a host of lesser luminaries played key roles in a struggle that was by no means conclusive. The United States' first Census in 1790 revealed that a quarter of the nation's rapidly-growing population – about a million people – spoke languages other than English. There were also already yawning gaps in pronunciation and usage among the new nation's English speakers. The idea of creating a uniquely American language, or at least an Americanized version of English, was therefore fraught with conflict that became even clearer as the nation expanded. Spelling would play a central role in a "War of the Dictionaries" a conflict considerably less bloody but sometimes almost as vicious as the then looming "War Between the States."

Chapter 2, "Can Anyone Spell 'Education?'" broadens the focus from tussles amongst nineteenth-century publishers and pedants to an exploration of how spelling was actually taught at the grass-roots. For years, most young Americans learned to read and spell in ill-equipped classrooms where both books and student attendance were often optional, and teachers of both sexes were poorly paid and frequently harassed. Yet, basic literacy, sometimes accompanied by spelling prowess, grew apace. Amid Northern antebellum enthusiasm for personal improvement and societal reform, superior and consistent spelling seemed an important key to the promise of success in America.

"Spelling Freedom," the third chapter, considers the special case of Southern spelling pedagogy before, during, and after the Civil War. A dearth of public schooling for poorer whites, coupled with ubiquitous laws designed to prevent literacy among slaves, made spelling a difficult yet intensely important achievement for both races. As war loomed, Southern publishers "borrowed" from Webster and infused some spellers with Confederate themes. Meanwhile, African-Americans risked beatings or much worse as they shared contraband Webster *Blue-Backs* before and even during the hostilities. Frederick Douglass and Booker T. Washington were but two of the more famous former slaves who would later recall their own struggles for literacy, sometimes assisted by educators, white and black, who brought spellers and other educational materials into the defeated South.

Well before the Civil War, some printers, stenographers, and professors had already envisioned and were soon actively promoting much more radical "reconstructions" of American and English orthography. Chapter 4, "The Peculiar Life and Near-Death of Spelling Reform," explores an array of efforts to reform or simplify spelling. The spelling simplification movement experienced its proudest hour and its worst setback in 1906 when President Theodore Roosevelt proposed to retool 3,000 words used in executive branch documents and correspondence. U. S. newspapers and many members of Congress ridiculed the coalition of English professors, philologists, and reformers, including Scottish-born industrialist Andrew Carnegie, who had helped to persuaded the Harvard-educated but spelling-challenged President to take this step.

Spelling bees were traditional rural pastimes, widely adopted in the nineteenth century by teachers searching for ways to lift the fog of indifference and boredom that afflicted one-room school houses and crowded urban classrooms alike. Chapter 5, "Bee Seasons," explores the peculiar concept of oral spelling competitions, divorced from spelling's primary and expanding role in service to accurate written communication. From its beginning in 1925, the competition known now as the Scripps National Spelling Bee, gathered finalists in Washington, D.C., seat of American power and patriotism. The Bee implicitly harked back to the nineteenth-century values of Webster and William Holmes McGuffey. Like the anti-evolutionary "Monkey Trial" in Tennessee that same year, the Bee, at least in its early years, helped to define what American children should, or should not, learn and believe.

The final chapter, "Spelling is Dead: Long Live Spelling!" brings spelling and its discontents into the twenty-first century. It asks questions about spelling ability and pedagogy in an age of spell-checkers, blogs, and "tweets." From the days of Webster, if not before, it has been popular to pin the blame for indifferent spelling performance on various controversial teaching methods that critics believe have ignored or defiled spelling education. Yet, there is little evidence that Americans today really spell much worse than their forebears did. Nor do they spell much better.

Indeed, concern for "proper" English has intensified in the current era. Traditionalists who home-school their children have made their mark at the National Bee. Facsimiles and reprints of spellers are popular with parents and antiquarians alike. Fears that spelling ability and accuracy are in peril are not limited to any particular ideology or creed. This means that the United States is still very far from finally eliminating what young Noah Webster called "all the trouble of spelling." For that, this dilatory author is decidedly grateful.

1 Young America's Spelling "Blues"

In August, 1841, Horace Mann, the best known educator in the United States, warned educators gathered in Boston that textbooks claiming to teach children how to spell were as dangerous as they were useless. He did not spare his ridicule. Noting that the shared Greek root for Orthography and Orthoepy – spelling and pronunciation – is defined as "straight" or "direct," he said, "If 'y,a,c,h,t,' is a straight or direct way of spelling yot…I hope we may be delivered from learning what crooked is." The vowels of the English language, he complained, "ought to be called five harlequins," since they collectively produce twenty-nine different sounds in speech. Instead, said Mann, reading and spelling "should be taught by giving them, not the common alphabetic sound, but the sounds which they are to have in combination – which is called the phonic or phonetic method; or, what I consider a far better and more philosophical mode, whole words should be taught before teaching the letters of which they are composed." He derided his era's customary rote chanting of the alphabet as "ventriloquism." The pleasures of language, Mann continued, are activated in the young by sensory experiences including color, melody, taste, and smell. As for traditional spelling texts, he added, even their paper exuded "odor and fungousness" so repulsive to students that "a soporific effluvium seems to emanate from the page…"

He was the state of Massachusetts' first public schools chief, soon to be acclaimed the father of American public education. His colorful denunciation, published as a forty-page booklet, was consistent with his lifelong abhorrence of traditional punishments inflicted on young learners by his era's "spare not the rod" school of pedagogy.

Not everyone agreed. In 1841, America's most successful spelling book was Noah Webster's, and he did not take kindly to Mann's or anyone else's criticisms. At age eighty-two, the grand old man of American English had just completed a second edition of his *An American Dictionary of the English Language*, twenty years in the making. A presentation copy was on its way to Britain's young Queen Victoria. Webster's various spellers for children, called "*Blue-Backs*" because they were bound inexpensively in bright blue paper, had been published since 1783, selling in numbers comparable only to the Bible. They would continue to do so for decades after his death in 1843. His followers, imitators, and rivals were legion. Nostalgic reminiscences by former users of Webster's *Blue-Back Speller* continued to appear in print well into the twentieth century.

Ever vigilant in defense of his copyrights and pedagogy, Webster was well aware of rumblings out of Boston and elsewhere. He encouraged his son-in-law, Amherst College professor William C. Fowler, husband to daughter Harriet, to defend him. "I have been struck with surprise," Webster wrote, "to see how men engaged in promoting education mistake the laws of the human mind. It is this mistake which has originated the scheme of teaching *spelling* and *definitions* at the same time." In a postscript, Webster expressed concern that Massachusetts rivals were scheming to "bring my elementary book into disrepute."

Webster and Mann's arms-length tussle over the correct way to introduce children to language skills continues to roil educational waters to this day. Yet the rival educators, despite their age gap, actually had a great deal in common. Mann's biographer describes young Horace, born in 1796, following his older sister Rebecca "about the house, holding a Noah Webster grammar in his hand, as she listened to his lesson while attending to her chores. Ostensibly, he was learning to spell..." Both men traced their ancestry to early New England Puritans, and were the sons of marginally successful farmers. Both overcame relative poverty to excel in college – Webster at Yale and Mann at Brown. Both trained as lawyers and had considerable success in attaining public positions. Both fended off accusations that their teaching methods and materials were insufficiently Christian to mold children into pious and God-fearing adults. Both were viewed as "radicals" who proposed to simplify the maddening orthography of the English language. And for both, but especially Webster, spelling and language were at the root of burgeoning nationalism. To pronounce like an American, to use American words and place-names, to *spell* like an American: these were necessary to complete the auspicious separation between Britain and the United States that the American Revolution had only begun. Encountering the alphabet and using its letters to make words remains the essential entry point without which higher realms of language and literacy would be even more problematic than they already were and are.

This would be no patriotic romp. As the Webster-Mann dispute suggests, a bitter battle for scholarly credibility and sales of spellers, grammars, and dictionaries had long been underway, and is indeed still with us. This earliest "National Spelling Bee" was a contest pitting politics, educational methods, Christian beliefs, and geographic regions. On two continents, patriots, pedants, and entrepreneurs staked claims to national pride, expertise, and profits. Language itself lay in the balance for this young nation that would by 1828 boast the world's largest English-speaking population.

Noah Webster's Domain

In the eighteenth century, and well beyond, English was a rowdy language that neither marched precisely across a printed page, nor flowed with perfect regularity from the lips of English speakers, be they Englishmen or colonials. Spelling was a wild frontier; even the best educated might spell erratically. Spelling in English attempts to accomplish tasks that do not easily coexist. Should spelling reflect etymology – where has a word come from and how has it changed? Must roots in Latin, French, Anglo-Saxon, or any other "original" language dictate modern English spelling? How about words of unknown, imprecise, or indeterminate origins, or borrowings from Hebrew, Arabic, Chinese, and other languages that do not use the Roman alphabet or any alphabet at all?

Or should spelling emerge from proper pronunciation? Noah

Webster would strive mightily but with scant success to make spelling into a tool that would perfectly align speech (which he called "prosody") with written English. In an era when oratory was more celebrated than words on paper, spelling was viewed primarily as a tool of sound, not sight. The proliferation of accents in "Englishes" spoken in the United States, United Kingdom, and across the globe reveal some of the pitfalls of privileging oral traditions over written language.

Yet, how truly reliable is the printed page? Can accurate and consistently spelled texts enable readers to better understand their language – or do they instead confuse when words spelled almost identically prove to have not only different meanings but often variant pronunciations? Can printers, typesetters, and proofreaders be trusted to produce correct orthography? The earliest American books were printed and bound in an arduous process that involved child labor, toxic inks, and heavy presses that could maim or cripple their operators. Even in the modern era of laser, offset, and ink jet printing, never mind "tweets," spelling mistakes regularly besmirch even professionally produced books and newspapers. In 2011, a *New York Times* opinionator would assail what she called a "typo explosion" caused by more errors perpetrated by fewer copy editors and slapdash spell checking that antagonizes careful readers and shrinks sales.

All of these issues gained traction as Enlightenment ideas of rationality, regularity, and order took hold among certain intellectual and social classes on both sides of the Atlantic. In the colonies, and later in the United States, literacy, including the idea of consistent and accurate spelling, was deeply enmeshed with hopes for American nationhood. Yearning for legitimacy and success, this experimental new nation had a lot to prove. It is no wonder, then, that language issues sparked "wars," and spelling became a commercial and ideological battlefield.

As was true of many innovations in eighteenth century America, the Americanization of spelling began with Benjamin Franklin, a New Englander who at age seventeen declared his own independence and became Philadelphia's adopted son and seer. As one of the colonies' more successful printers, Franklin was among those who helped to decide what books from abroad would be read by literate Americans, and which homegrown literary undertakings would reach colonial audiences. In 1747, Franklin's press began publishing Britain's most popular "speller" for children, authored by Thomas Dilworth, a clergyman and schoolmaster from Wapping, a Thames-side neighborhood in Greater London. Although his book ignored American places and peoples, Dilworth's *A New Guide to the English Tongue* soon led the field among many similar imports from the Mother Country.

A year later, David Hall, Franklin's chosen successor, published Englishman George Fisher's manual for aspiring businessmen, *The American Instructor, or Young Man's Beſt Companion,* already in its seventh London edition. This version proclaimed itself "better adapted to these American colonies, than any other book of the like kind." Fisher's sage advice went through at least thirty-one editions, outlasting its author, the American Revolution, and the so-called "long s" or "esh" (ſ), which made spelling even more peculiar in the eighteenth century than it would soon be in the nineteenth. Fisher's first chapter, "To Spell, Read, and Write True English," asserts, "...for let a Perſon write never ſo good a Hand, yet if he be defective in Spelling, he will be ridiculed and contemptibly ſmiled at, notwithſtanding his fair Writing; and which will indeed make his Orthographical Faults be more conspicuous." This was no idle warning. "That [George] Washington was not a schollar [sic] is certain," John Adams would tell his friend and fellow patriot Benjamin Rush years later. "That he was too illiterate, unlearned, and unread for his station and reputation is equally past dispute." However, Adams, who admired Washington for many other reasons, was appalled when Timothy Pickering, a key member of Washington's (and later Adams') cabinet, twice went out of his way to tell Adams that the nation's first President was an ignoramus who "could not write a sentence without misspelling some word."

By 1768, Benjamin Franklin, as Pennsylvania's colonial agent, was in London, caught up in efforts to mend relations between Parliament and colonials seething over the recent Stamp Act fiasco. Yet he found time to critique English spelling in a pamphlet titled, A *Scheme for a new Alphabet and a reformed Mode of Spelling*. It was eventually published in America in 1779. Franklin proposed to banish from the alphabet six letters he considered redundant (c, j, q, u, w, and y) while adding six new characters that he claimed would better represent the language's actual sounds. The *j* in Benjamin would be replaced with a new letter that looked like a large *S* and sounded like *ish*. He tried to clarify vowel pronunciations by developing his own symbols, and tested his new alphabetic scheme in correspondence with Mary (Polly) Stevenson, a dear London friend. Miss Stevenson was underwhelmed, replying archly that she could "si meni" problems with Franklin's reforms. A twentieth century linguist who analyzed Franklin's bold plan called it "highly creditable" but observed that America's seer was known to pronounce *frind* for friend, *git* for get.

In the 1780s, the aged Franklin and young Noah Webster developed a mutually rewarding relationship. Webster had early mastered the art of flattery, exercising his skills on some of the most important men of his era while making himself important as well. He was, in a word, a toady, albeit a talented and industrious one. In pursuit of copyright protection for what would soon become his spelling book, Webster even offered to tutor George Washington's step-grandchildren, although, if we believe Pickering and Adams, lessons for Grandpa might have proved more useful. This plan fell through when Webster realized that working for the father of his country would leave scant time for his own expansive literary labors.

Webster truly admired Franklin's genius and enthusiasm. But the young New Englander was also not averse to the prospect that endorsement by this American icon would elevate both his own national reputation and his sales. He took a keen interest in the elder statesman's spellings and included some of Franklin's language ideas in a revised edition of his speller. Webster's main work as both writer and sycophant focused on a publishing project designed to be as profitable as it was virtuous. He set forth his plan in 1782 when he petitioned Connecticut's General Assembly for a thirteen-year copyright to justify the financial risk of undertaking to publish and sell a "proper spelling book." Unlike Dilworth's lists of British towns that Webster found "totally useless in America," his book would include "a short account of the discovery of America" and other features designed to instill education, morality, and patriotism. His book, he said, would "promote the interest of literature and the honor and dignity of the American empire." The letter was respectful yet assertive; the young schoolmaster made a patriotic statement, quite possibly inadvertently, by writing "honor" instead of the standard "honour." Dilworth's book, printed in England, used -our endings and other spellings that had been enshrined in British lexicographer Dr. Samuel Johnson's 1755 dictionary.

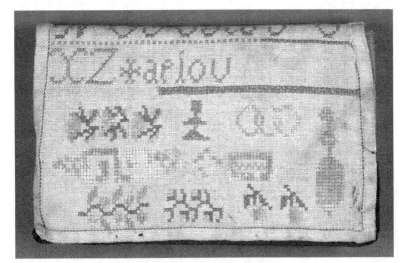

Gussy Up Your *Blue-Back*

A year later, Webster published his first speller (pedantically titled *A Grammatical Institute of the English Language, Part I,* at the behest of yet another influential mentor, Yale College president Ezra Stiles. Within months, the first five thousand copies had sold out. Renamed *The American Spelling Book* in 1787, Webster's little text became an even greater success. By 1803, Webster was claiming three million in circulation.

Soon this struggling young man of twenty-four was poised to make himself, as some later biographers call him, "schoolmaster to America." He was one of throngs of young men and a few women who were embarking on what soon became a crowded, cutthroat, and thriving trade in textbooks and educational materials. Webster's fame, or at least his name, endures largely because he was overall more ambitious and visionary than his rivals. He pioneered the use of "celebrity" endorsements and traveled tirelessly hawking his wares. One such trip began in Hartford in May 1785 and took him, via ship, horseback, and carriage on the most rudimentary roads as far as Charleston, South Carolina. Lecturing and showering school administrators and local dignitaries with examination copies at every stop, Webster did not return home until November 1786. A month after his twenty-eighth birthday, he was beginning to wonder when he would ever find the time and resources to marry. Not until 1789 was he at last able to wed Rebecca Greenleaf.

Armed with political connections and some copyright protection, Webster saw before him a new nation thirsting for knowledge befitting the world's first large republic; a nation that was already attracting immigrants from both English and non-English-speaking countries. He would regularly enlist his growing family – especially his sons-in-law – to promote his books and defend their academic superiority. Webster was without peer when it came to using ridicule, allegations of plagiarism, and attacks on rivals' patriotism to assure his dominance as a publisher of educational materials. In the contentious and tendentious world of the early American Republic, Noah Webster fit right in. He would reap what he had sown, making enemies, and hovering near bankruptcy on many occasions, yet ultimately prevailing, even beyond his own death.

Spelling's path to "Americanism" was as twisted as it was ferocious. Treating the English language as personal property to be dominated, pacified, and possessed, rather than the birthright of all English speakers, publishers, scholars, and teachers regularly asserted their own correctness and patriotism by claiming exclusive rights to certain words and phrases while scorning spellings perceived as eccentric, imaginative, or favored by competitors. Spellers offered by Webster and his many rivals and imitators bore little resemblance to modern spelling dictionaries, workbooks, or electronic spelling programs. Rather, they are examples of what modern experts call the Alphabet Method of reading instruction or "spelling-for-reading." The first pages of virtually every speller of the era laid out the English alphabet, rendered in upper and lower case, and in both Roman and italic fonts. Once students had memorized all twenty-six letters in order and could spell each letter's name (*ay, bee, cee*, and so on) their instructors would grill them endlessly on word tables, starting with nonsense syllables and eventually evolving into actual words, chosen less for meaning, information, or context than for their syllabic complexity and varied stresses or accents. Later, some rudimentary fables and uplifting stories might round out the lesson plan. Despite the quaint charm that some still seem to find in these old schoolbooks (as evidenced by the impressive number of facsimiles and original editions currently offered by Amazon and elsewhere) they remained, as Horace Mann suggested in 1841, badly bound, cheaply printed, and deeply boring.

By 1850, the United States would boast an English language "recognizably its own," but the creation of a language that might be called "American" was hard-fought at every turn, proving, in the words of one modern scholar that it was "more difficult to declare independence from Samuel Johnson than it had been to reject King George III." That Dr. Johnson had in 1775 published a savage critique of American independence only raised the linguistic and patriotic stakes. Partisanship of many kinds infected and inflected spelling, reading, and education, tending to follow regional lines and strongly shaped by differences in educational achievement and political and religious affiliations.

Although New England led the way in literacy and was a hotbed of these early controversies, competing ideas about America's literacy needs followed settlers across an expanding nation. There was, for example, a Cincinnati bloc that included many transplanted New Englanders, including sisters Catharine Beecher and Harriet Beecher Stowe, their father, the renowned minister Lyman Beecher, and Harriet's husband Calvin, a Biblical scholar. In 1831, the young French observer Alexis de Tocqueville visited Cincinnati, America's "gateway to the West." He found a raw and roaring hog-butchering city of thirty thousand that had doubled its population in just the past five years and was scrambling to lure sufficient teachers for its growing network of public schools.

Cincinnati's booming economy was also attracting the likes of New Yorker Albert Picket who had published his first *Juvenile Spelling Book* in 1808, promising that no word would appear that was "not consonant with the purity of religion and morality." When Cincinnati's schools picked Picket's speller for their students, Noah Webster accused that author of presumptuous plagiarism. He encouraged William Webster, his own son and feckless business agent, to spread these allegations in the local press. The younger Webster did so, with scant success. However, Cincinnati brothers Alexander and William Holmes McGuffey, whose appealing primers and readers would soon begin to dominate American juvenile education, managed to avert Webster's wrath by adopting much of the orthography of his *Blue-Back* spellers, thus virtually assuring continued sales of Webster's most profitable educational publication.

Emerging from New York's rural Finger Lakes region, a teacher and author named Lyman Cobb would become Webster's most irritating commercial rival, torturing the old man at every turn. In 1831, Cobb collected years of complaint into a colorfully-bound fifty-six page booklet, printed in a typeface so tiny that it was a wonder that any one bothered to read it. Forty-two years younger than Webster, Cobb was the product of humble country schools. By age sixteen, he had metamorphosed from pupil to instructor in a log schoolhouse in Slatersville, then, as now, a tiny farm community. Using Webster's speller as his model, Cobb in 1821 published the first edition of what would become known as "Cobb's Speller." Lacking any formal higher education, the young author styled himself as a "Philomath" or lover of knowledge. His book, printed in nearby Ithaca, was a great success, with several editions eventually selling about four million copies and enabling Cobb to become a respected figure in New York City, despite bad business decisions that seem to have left him perpetually broke. He would die a pauper in 1864.

Cobb had not graduated from or even attended Yale or any other university, but his instincts as a teacher and author tended toward the more grandiose of British language traditions, represented for many years with great success by John Walker, an English actor turned elocutioner and lexicographer who had died in 1807. Cobb made correct pronunciation a central selling point of his *A Just Standard for Pronouncing the English Language*, and boasted that his text was "calculated to teach the orthography of Walker." (Albert Picket made similar claims). That, and his surprising success, at once put Cobb at loggerheads with Webster.

From a modern perspective, it might seem that devotees of these archrivals – the deceased Walker channeled by Lyman Cobb versus the living Noah Webster – shared some exceedingly important goals. Both camps aimed to teach children to pronounce properly, thereby hoping to overcome enormous class distinctions that in Britain doomed Cockneys and other less educated speakers, as well as Scots, Irish, and the Welsh, to scorn and social marginalization. Likewise, Webster sought to protect his new nation from splintering linguistically into self-defeating regionalisms and dialects. As Webster explained, his spelling book was meant "to destroy the provincial prejudices that originate in the trifling differences of dialect..." These, he feared, might do grievous damage to the "harmony of the United States."

Webster and most of his rivals believed that the central purpose of spelling was to instill uniformly excellent speech in all social classes – but whose spelling would prevail? Webster, who scorned what he deemed the outworn and affected pronunciations of the erstwhile Mother Country, demanded a truly American vocabulary, and pronunciation, emerging from proper spelling. Inevitably, Webster would favor the accents of his Connecticut upbringing

The idea that Britain and the United States are "two nations separated by a common language" (generally attributed to George Bernard Shaw, an ardent spelling reformer) is today a humorous commonplace, but the process of differentiation in which Webster and Cobb (along with many others) played key roles, was seriously contentious. Cobb's 1831 pamphlet detailing Webster's flaws is titled *A Critical Review of the Orthography of Dr. Webster's Series of Books for Systematick Instruction in the English Language....* Cobb's use of "Systematick" — already considered a quaint spelling — was but one clue that an entire can of orthographical worms had been opened.

In this era of growth and flux, many Americans were reconciled with Britain's "mother tongue" while "patriots" were just as happy denouncing British spelling as pretentious or outmoded. In a 1990 essay, "Errours and Endeavors," English professor Chris M. Anson evaluated the politics of replacing *-our* endings with *-or*, in words like honor and savior, and suggested strong implications for other significant spelling shifts. These include *-re/er* (as in theater) *-ise/ize* (as in Americanize but not surprise or analyze); *-exion/ection* (as in connection) and *-ck/c* endings (such as Lyman Cobb's "systematick") most of which continue today to distinguish British and American spelling.

The *-our* ending had been fading in British usage, Anson notes, until Dr. Johnson, who "had no formal system whatsoever for the spelling of these words," resuscitated it in his 1755 dictionary and retained in his final revision of 1773. Webster's first speller, the *Grammatical Institute*, "generally" adopted the orthography of Dr. Johnson and, in an example of inconsistency that would have delighted his many rivals, the same Noah Webster who invoked "honor " when asking Connecticut for copyright protection in 1782, used the words "honour," "errour," and "favourable" a year later.

Assailing Webster for caprice, contradiction, and presumed character flaws, Cobb claimed to have identified 1,200 discrepancies in Webster's recently-published *American Dictionary*, and he compiled an eight-page chart to demonstrate Webster's spelling irregularities across the array of his publications since 1806. Cobb intimated that Webster's success arose from years of fawning on important politicians and academics. And, as Cobb revealed darkly, the most recent Webster speller, his *Elementary Spelling Book*, was actually "compiled by Aaron Ely, and published under the name of Noah Webster LL.D." The upstart Cobb was baldly suggesting that Webster must be in his dotage.

It is only a slight exaggeration to assert that Webster avoided senility even after his death, which occurred on May 28, 1843 as he held a copy of his speller in his hand. Meanwhile, he was very much alive to counter Cobb's claims and complaints. Never naming the younger man, whom he considered to be almost illiterate, Webster instead focused his ire on the two deceased English sages, John Walker and Dr. Johnson, whom he accused of making the already disorderly and inconsistent English language even "more corrupt." Webster also seized the opportunity to mention that his forthcoming dictionary would purify the language, laying a strong foundation "for something like regularity and system in orthography, pronunciation, and construction."

Yet Webster also admitted to difficulties in making English pronunciation and spelling behave with any consistency at all. Even esteemed writers (including himself) said Webster, erratically spell such words as "risk and risque; civilize and civilise; surprise and surprize...Differences of these and similar kinds now occur to the number of thousands in the *best* authors, and were so familiar to me that, in correcting the proof sheets, some of them escaped me and the gentlemen who assisted me." It was an unusually frank admission, a rare *mea culpa* by a man of iron certitude.

As controversial as Webster remained all his life, few of his ideas maddened his many rivals more than his adventures in radical spelling reform. Beneath his Federalist propriety and midlife religious piety beat the heart of a man who championed "rude" speech and insisted that spelling was too difficult for most Americans to master. Even Benjamin Franklin, Webster's first mentor in language innovation, clung to some endearing peculiarities of then-standandard English. The elderly but always engaged seer told Webster that "we should endeavour [note the British spelling] to remove all the difficulties, however small, that discourage the learning of [our language]." But he also deplored printers' rapidly-advancing inclination to eliminate the antiquated long esh (ſ), familiar even today from the Declaration of Independence that Franklin had signed just thirteen years earlier. "Certainly the omitting this prominent letter makes a line appear more even, but renders it less immediately legible; as the paring of men's noses might smooth and level their faces..." wrote Franklin. It was their last exchange: on April 17 Franklin died at eighty-four. A final letter from his eager acolyte was in the mail.

Smoothing and leveling (and tweaking noses) were just the beginning of Webster's reformist ambitions, although he prudently kept his most extreme ideas out of his spellers. In 1789, as the United States adopted its Constitution of which he was a strong advocate, Webster had laid out the "Necessity, Advantages and Practicability of Reforming the Mode of Spelling." It appeared as an appendix to his personal declaration of independence from the presumably corrupted language of Britain. "The que*ſ*tion now occurs; ought the Americans to retain the*ſe* faults...or ought they at once to reform the*ſe* abuses and introduce order and regularity into the orthography of the AMERICAN TONGUE?" he demanded. His plan encompassed both spelling simplifications and more radical changes. These included omitting all "superfluous or silent letters; as the *a* in *bread*"; using "trifling alterations" such as textual dots and slashes to pin down vowel sounds, and excising "more vague and indeterminate" Greek and French influences on English spelling. This would require, for example, replacing the Greek-derived "chorus" with *korus* and the French "oblique" with *obleek*.

At last, said Webster, children would actually learn to spell, since "[i]t would ...be as difficult to spell wrong, as it is now to spell right." At last, foreigners and Americans of all social conditions would easily read and pronounce every word as the chasm between written and spoken language was erased. Cleansed of useless silent letters, books would be shorter and cheaper. But most importantly, said Webster, this new national language, which the British would never deign to adopt, would become America's invincible "band of *national union...*"

In Webster's "Collection of Essays...on Moral, Historical, Political and Literary" titled *Fugitiv Writings, fugitive*'s final "e" was not just silent but had apparently run away, while the silent "W" in "writing" stubbornly remained. This ambitious compilation of recent essays, many originally written under pseudonyms, attracted such subscribers as then Vice President John Adams and thirteen members of Congress, but disappointingly failed to lure enough notables to offset Webster's publication costs.

Although most of these essays were orthographically orthodox, complete with "eshes," two of Webster's essays promised more shocking spelling breakthroughs. These included *k* standing in for the hard "c" and flurries of *z*'s in place of "s" in words like *as* and *is*. Wrote Webster: "Every possible reezon...for altering the spelling of wurds, stil exists in full force; and if a gradual reform should not be made in our language, it wil proov that we are less under the influence of reezon than our ancestors." (Here, "full" oddly retains its traditional complement of two -l's).

In his 1806 *Compendious Dictionary of the English Language*, Webster again blamed the Norman French conquest of 1066 for "corrupting" English's "genuine spellings" and attempting to "crush the Saxon and obliterate their language." He surely intended his readers to compare these ancient acts of linguistic cleansing to British offenses against American speech and spellings, and similar sins perpetrated by their Anglophile kin in the United States. The ancient fissure between the conflicting halves of the English language - Anglo-Saxon and Norman French - remains a major reason why English spelling is so complicated. Despite the mockery of many learned Americans, a struggle over "learned" words and ordinary ones (predominately Anglo-Saxon) would consume the energies of some of America's most esteemed educators, English professors, and philologists into the twentieth century where spelling reform would reach its crescendo. "so overemphasized the connection of English and Anglo-Saxon that it took fifty years or more to recover."

Born in 1777, John Pickering, the son of Timothy Pickering, Webster's patron and confirmed spelling snob, was weaned on Webster's first speller but became one of his more scathing critics. Even at age five, John rarely erred when "spelling...a word he has once read," even before his doting father a year later furnished his first-born with Noah Webster's new offering. This first speller, wrote the elder Pickering, was "ingenious, and at the same time easy," and would foster "elegant pronunciation." Thus schooled, the precocious John grew up to become a lawyer and brilliant amateur philologist with Anglophilic tendencies cemented by his residence in London from 1799 to 1801. Young Pickering himself consistently "favoured" the spellings prescribed in Dr. Johnson's dictionary. Nor was he was at all shy about the presumed deficiencies of his own nation's literary culture. In 1816, he published a 206-page collection of suspect Americanisms, most of which he deemed "provincial," "barbarous," or at best "peculiar." He denounced the "thirsty reformers" and "presumptuous" American phrasemakers whose "passion for senseless novelties" threatened to turn English into an "American Tongue" that might "unsettle the whole of our admirable language." This trend, Pickering warned, might even compromise Americans' continuing ability to read the best English authors. A great many of Pickering's examples of what was uncouth or just plain wrong with America's evolving usage, speech, and spelling were plucked directly from Noah Webster's first stab at dictionary-making, his 1806 "Compendious" dictionary.

Webster responded to Pickering with his own sixty-page rejoinder that mixed high dudgeon and the pathos of a great man misunderstood and underestimated. The "English themselves are chargeable with most of the anomalies and barbarisms in our language," he declared, adding several sour comments on British spelling practices, including the hated Johnsonian final *k* in public, music, or systematic. Webster ended on a maudlin note, styling himself, at age fifty-eight, as poor and all but forgotten, even though, he stressed, "I have contributed, to a small degree, to the instruction of at least four millions of the rising generation; and it is not unreasonable to expect that a few seeds of improvement planted by my hand may germinate and ripen into valuable fruit, when my remains shall be mingled with the dust." This obvious reference to his *Blue-Backs* cast young Pickering, once his star student, as an ungrateful germinated seed.

Neither man backed down. Pickering continued to condemn Americanized English, while Webster went on to complete his much larger and even more controversial *An American Dictionary of the English Language.* When Pickering was asked by two Boston editors in 1829 to review this new Webster work, so that "we...ourselves exhibit the errors of Webster before they fall under the acrid pens of the European critics," he twice declined. Regarding Webster's word choices, a modern scholar would sum up, "for the general public clearly the most controversial feature...was its simplified spelling." Confronted with such words as "tung" and "wimen," New York newspapers in particular accused Webster of "unsettling the language."

Soon a rancorous "War of the Dictionaries" would be reaching its zenith, and, while focused on dictionaries, would frequently descend into the mud of spelling. It raged for more than thirty years, outliving both Noah Webster and Joseph E. Worcester, its marquee combatants. As a contest over sales, intellectual capital, and truly American values, this "war" oddly paralleled the nation's looming Civil War. This is not to suggest that the merits or deficiencies of a book, even one as important as an American dictionary, equals the political and moral issues at stake in the war that tore the United States apart. But it does help us understand the passions and anxieties of this fledgling nation, and testifies to the central importance of language in creating and maintaining a viable polity, or failing to do so.

Neither Webster nor Worcester could claim to be the United States' first native-born lexicographer. That distinction belonged to the providentially named Samuel Johnson Jr., who was the son of a Guilford, Connecticut clothing maker, and no known relation of the famous British sage, Dr. Johnson. It seems likely that Johnson Jr., a village schoolteacher who prepared his book in collaboration with local minister John Elliott, benefited from this name confusion when he published this first dictionary in 1798. A second edition of Johnson's brief *School Dictionary*, slightly enlarged, came out in 1800, promising to deliver "the choicest words found in the best English authors." In other words, this dictionary was American-made, but had little uniquely American content. That same year, Caleb Alexander's assertively-titled *Columbian Dictionary of the English Language*, which included such obvious Americanisms as "Congressional" was deemed "presumptuous" and "disgusting" by many American critics. Linguistic Americanism was in the air but many of the nation's best educated men and women still clung fervently to British models of usage, speech, and spelling.

By the time the "Dictionary Wars" erupted, scholar Joseph Emerson Worcester had become a bridge figure between committed Anglophiles and the American "radicalism" of Noah Webster. Worcester would say years later that he had made a grievous mistake in 1828 when he was cajoled into preparing an abridged version of Noah Webster's new *American Dictionary*. The fee – $2,000 – was ample but it seriously complicated Worcester's future life and career. In his own *Dictionary of the English Language* of 1860, posthumously reissued in 1876, a biographical sketch lamented Worcester's mistake. "Subsequent events vindicated his instinctive disinclination to the task, and caused him to regret that he had not persevered in his original refusal..." Chauncey Goodrich, a Yale professor of rhetoric and husband of Webster's daughter Julia, had once thanked Worcester for his editing labors, saying "This gives me and Mr. Webster's other friends the highest satisfaction; for there is no man in the United States...who would be equally acceptable." These were the last kind words ever exchanged between the Webster and Worcester camps. In fact, Webster later wrote this son-in-law out of his will, partly for his failure to properly supervise young Worcester.

Born in Bedford, New Hampshire in 1784, Worcester was the second son and one of fifteen children of Jesse and Sarah Parker Worcester. His father and all but one of Joseph's siblings taught school when they were not farming. Two of Joseph's paternal uncles became prominent ministers. A cousin, Samuel Austin Worcester, was a missionary to the Cherokee who championed the tribe's own "Syllabary,"a system for writing the Cherokee language, partly inspired by Webster's spellers, over John Pickering's alphabetic scheme. Yet the family was far from wealthy. Despite his "quiet and unwearied perseverance and resolute energy," not until age twenty-five did Joseph, "with much difficulty," persuade Yale to admit him. Apparently, Yale was no longer the relatively hospitable institution that another farmer's son, Noah Webster, had entered in 1774 at age sixteen. After graduation, Worcester taught in Salem, Massachusetts, where future author Nathaniel Hawthorne was among his students.

(Hawthorne would later join Horace Mann, his brother-in-law, in praising Worcester's dictionary). In 1828, settled in Cambridge, Worcester began preparing new editions of other authors' dictionaries, both British and American, including the fateful Webster work-for-hire.

Webster was a pugnacious patriarch who loved a good fight; Worcester seems to have been a shy scholar with "habits of quiet research," who married Amy Elizabeth McKean, a Harvard professor's daughter, when she was forty and he fifty-seven. Even after he was afflicted in 1847 by cataracts that destroyed the sight in his right eye and required five operations to save the other, Worcester soldiered on with his lexicographic scholarship, acquiring a circle of Cambridge friends and admirers, and a publisher prepared to trumpet the superiority of his dictionary.

The Dictionary Wars focused on etymology, but spelling issues resonated with both young spellers and their teachers. At the most basic level, using a dictionary requires the seeker to locate the word, and that entails knowing how to spell it. Worcester published his own *Comprehensive Pronouncing and Explanatory Dictionary of the English Language* in 1830. Using English models of spelling and pronunciation, although not slavishly, Worcester's tome was unlikely to gratify Webster. Associates of both men piled on, employing the customary disparaging letters and articles, many anonymous or written by surrogates and placed in accommodating publications. For almost five months, beginning in November 1834, readers of the Worcester (Mass). *Palladium* were assailed by competing claims.

The melee began with an unsigned attack on Joseph Worcester in the weekly *Palladium*. Soon, the warring lexicographers had become regular contributors. Writing from New Haven on January 25, 1835, Webster made his strongest accusation. "Sir," he wrote unkindly, "Before I saw [in the *Palladium*] a charge against you of committing plagiarism on my Dictionary, I had not given much attention to your Dictionary." Webster then laid exclusive claim to 121 entries – many considered Americanisms, including "spry," "tomato," "slump," "emphasize," and "tirade." He challenge Worcester to explain how he came to appropriate these words for his own work.

Worcester's equally frosty reply was posted from Cambridge on February 6. "Though I have no love of contention," he wrote, "yet if I must be dragged into a newspaper controversy in defence of myself in this matter, I should prefer that, of all men in the world, it should be with yourself, writing under your own name." He implicitly accused Webster of inadequate scholarship as he attributed virtually all of the words at issue to various American and British compilations, some dating back a century or more. Words commonly used in print or in speech, Worcester asserted, belong "not exclusively to any individual, but to all who write and speak the language."

By 1850, the Dictionary Wars were again in full cry. As sectional politics roiled both the nation and academia, friends and critics of both dictionaries chose sides. By then, of course, Webster was ten years dead, but his heirs, led by western Massachusetts publishers George and Charles Merriam, zealously took up the fight.

The firm that would create a dictionary empire began commercial printing in 1797 on a hand press once owned by Benjamin Franklin. Like most printers of their era, the Merriams focused on educational and religious books and tracts, sometimes adding more spicy material, including slave and Indian captivity narratives and novels. In 1804, they had published an unlicensed version of Webster's current speller, but backed off quickly when the author complained of copyright infringement. Soon after Webster's death, the Merriams were chosen to carry on the publication of his *American Dictionary*, amid Webster family controversy. In 1857, the Merriams obtained rights to the Webster *Spellers* as well.

The two dense and expensive volumes of Webster's dictionary had not exactly been flying off bookshop shelves. Detractors, soon to include supporters of Joseph Worcester, derisively called the dictionary "Noah's Ark", so stuffed they said it was with suspect etymologies, "vulgar" spellings, and many words that Webster claimed as his own coinages. For generations, said a later author, Boston and Harvard elites scorned to "open the pages of Webster without a well-bred shudder."

The Merriams made two crucial business decisions. They squeezed the dictionary into a single volume while dropping its price from twenty to six dollars– still expensive but now within the means of many middle-class readers and schoolmasters. They also hired a group of distinguished scholars, most of them affiliated with Yale, and headed by Webster's disowned but highly respected and quite conventional son-in-law Chauncey Goodrich. This team would revise Webster's big book in ways that would eventually turn this quirky and sometimes maddening life's work of an aging and stubborn author into an authoritative and indispensable reference.

Equally important were the Merriams' marketing methods in the face of Worcester's very credible challenge. Using the latest promotional techniques, Merriam sales agents used large, attractive posters to persuade school boards to adopt Webster's dictionary. By the 1850s, public schools in New York, Massachusetts, and New Jersey had purchased thousands for their classrooms. The Merriams also marshaled rapturous endorsements, mainly from politicians and newspaper editors, and even a few who were deceased. Praise from President James K. Polk, Zachary Taylor, the Mexican War hero and future President, and more than thirty U. S. Senators poured forth. The Merriam forces even intimated that Worcester's friends, concentrated in the Whig/Republican stronghold of Boston, were actively anti-Southern and sworn enemies of the Democratic Party. Southerners, according to one historian, "took seriously the charge that Webster was a Yankee reformer," and, with public education lagging badly in their region, state officials in the soon-to-be Confederacy were rarely able or willing to allocate funds for dictionaries.

Meanwhile, Worcester was attracting the support of eastern academics and intellectuals, including Horace Mann, Thomas Gallaudet (himself a speller author, later best known as an educator of the deaf), poet William Cullen Bryant, orator Edward Everett

Hale, and physician Oliver Wendell Holmes, who once joked that
Boston literary men called to court could, "by special statute," testify
using Worcester's dictionary in place of the Holy Bible. In 1856, a
presidential election year in which the fate of the Union loomed large,
New York's nationally-circulated *United States Democratic Review*
found space in four monthly issues to allow critics and champions
of the late Noah Webster and his heirs to debate his orthography.
Best-known for its espousal of "Manifest Destiny" during its 1840s
heyday under editor John L. O'Sullivan, the *Democratic Review* in
1856 remained an influential, if financially struggling, periodical
edited by Spencer W. Cone, a Virginia-born lawyer and poet who
had been a long-time contributor.

This "Spell-Off" began in the March issue when Edward S.
Gould mounted an often wickedly witty attack on the most recent
edition of Webster's *American Dictionary*. Webster, said Gould, was
a radical who "aspired to a Newtonian law that would reconcile all
orthographical inconsistencies; he produced certain arbitrary rules of
his own creation that...are whimsically limited in their scope, and are
ridiculous from their reciprocal contradictions," later adding, "the
lexicographer's inconsistency approaches the sublime!"

Gould was a famously arrogant language "purist" who generally
disdained Americanized literature and speech. Born in Connecticut,
he dabbled at play writing in New York. He later authored a highly
prescriptive grammar and was an advocate of British-inflected spelling. In that connection, he chastised the Merriam firm for intro-
ducing "Webster's spelling into their books, probably as a matter of
contract; and some newspapers have, to a greater or less extent, taken
the same course. But these instances carry no authority...Educated
men and good writers, generally, have repudiated the experiment."

An anonymous champion took Webster's side in the June issue. The fourteen-page response, titled "Battle of the Books," was
preceded by an editor's note framing the stakes of this debate about
spelling. "For ourselves, we frankly admit, that our sympathies are
rather anti-Websterian than otherwise....We owe it to the importance

of the issue raised...to examine the arguments...with a calm impartiality." Describing Gould as "shut in by an ultra conservatism," this advocate defended Webster's efforts to reform English, while admitting that the job was not yet completed. For centuries, he wrote, English orthography "was confused and unsettled" with "every man...'his own speller.' Simplification, said this author, "has never been regular or systematic. Every gain has been made at the expense of much remaining irregularity; and there have always been persons ready to object to all reforms on this account."

The article took up Gould's criticisms in detail, sifting every -re/-er, double l, and -our/-or. Despite the "cheap rhetoric of sneers" directed at Webster, his legacy shall prevail, his prophetic champion asserted. The old man's fame, he said, increases yearly, illumining "the first gropings of knowledge in many millions of children....It has dignified American scholarship, and made American authority in the republic of letters more felt and respected."

It was a patriotic reminder of both the power and limits of language as the nation itself fractured. After running another set of anti- and pro-Webster articles in July and August, editor Cone had enough. "It is, perhaps, unnecessary for us to add that here, as to this magazine, this discussion must terminate," he wrote. By July 1857, the *Democratic Review* was under new management; two years later it was defunct.

The spelling brawl that raged within the Dictionary War would outlast it. Critics of Noah Webster had been most annoyed by his periodic claims to have created a truly American orthography and to have imposed real consistency in spelling and pronunciation. Both claims were almost too easy to dispute, whether leveled by commercial rivals like Lyman Cobb, or by more learned critics. Said an anonymous *New York Times* reviewer of Worcester's dictionary in May, 1860: "Spelling is a matter for a volume in quarto. There always have been rebels to the orthographic rules...in the early ages of English there were no rules...an author often spelling a word a dozen ways on the same page...[T]he fatal mistake which Dr.

Webster made was his assumption that he had a mission to *regulate* the English language rather than simply recording it."

Worcester too acknowledged the unsettled state of spelling, saying in his new edition that orthography was "an evil...which is unavoidable, and to which living languages are generally more or less subject." Worcester conceded the *–our/or* debate to the Websterites, saying, "the prevailing usage in the United States, if not the most unexceptional, is the most convenient."

The onset of Civil War in April, 1861 diverted energies from the protracted Dictionary War. The Merriams suffered business setbacks when war commanded other priorities in the North, and their already meager Southern market seceded. In 1864, the Boston-based *Atlantic Monthly* published a surprisingly laudatory review of the newest Webster dictionary, while still finding fault with remaining "peculiarities of spelling which are commonly known as Websterianisms..." In closing, the reviewer called a truce in this time of war, saying, "Let there be no new War of the Dictionaries. The world is wide enough for both..."

Six months after the Confederacy's surrender in 1865, Worcester died, leaving behind a dictionary that remained a viable competitor into the early twentieth century, even though it lacked the corporate muscle that the long-dead Webster still enjoys. Meanwhile, those millions of American children, some equipped with *Blue-Backs* and dictionaries, and many more lacking, were "groping" with the myriad difficulties of spelling. Their struggles and those of their parents, teachers, and textbook purveyors command attention.

2 | *Can Anyone Spell "Education?"*

Who is the worst speller in American history? It's a tough call, but William Clark is a leading contender. Best known as Meriwether Lewis's partner in the 1804-1806 exploration of the Louisiana Purchase, Clark, a tough and resourceful soldier and frontiersman, is nearly as celebrated in literary and linguistic circles as the most creative speller (and misspeller) ever. The editor of the definitive Lewis and Clark journals has hailed Clark and his company's "erratic, but delightful and ingenious, manner of spelling," and a Lewis and Clark chronicler dubbed Clark the "master misspeller of them all."

Clark's defenders assert that his irregular orthography (shared to some degree by most members of his and Lewis's Corps of Discovery) was a reasonable response to shifting patterns in American language and pronunciation. Only inventive spelling could effectively convey the new peoples, plants, animals, and topography that made the expedition so important. And, far from being "erratic," Clark's linguistic champions contend, the expedition's journalers made sense, if not standardization, by aptly invoking current spelling trends, employing phonics, and making reasonable analogies to words with which they were already familiar. Though these journals are "chaotic, defenders finds important clues to the sounds of Virginian English at the turn of the first truly American century.'

But when does "invented spelling" go too far? Clark's four versions of "mosquito," none correct by today's standard, and his twenty-seven variations on "Sioux" are more understandable than his egregious misspellings of the sixth day of the week – "Satday," "Sattarday," Satterday, and "Saturday." Was Clark entirely untutored, merely an indifferent student, or a sorry example of the state of American education? As the youngest son in a large Virginia family who migrated to the Kentucky frontier, William Clark, born in 1770, missed out on the formal education afforded his older brothers, including Revolutionary War hero George Rogers Clark. William was nearly full-grown by the time Noah Webster began offering his spellers. Clark would go on to excel at maps and calculations, less so with books. Educated at home, Clark "learned to read and write but apparently never settled on a consistent manner of spelling..." This life-long proclivity would often embarrass him in an era when even federal clerks would snicker at poor penmanship, never mind bad spelling. Clark's spelling improved over the years, but he continued to rely on better-schooled colleagues, including young Nicholas Biddle, a well-born and college-educated Philadelphian who wrote an official history of the Corps of Discovery and often vetted Clark's reports before they were made public.

Even Clark's boss, Thomas Jefferson, America's foremost wordsmith, was known to employ "inconsistent and even whimsical spellings," including "independant," and he regularly spelled "honor," minus the Johnsonian *u*, before Noah Webster made that missing letter a badge of true American spelling. Yet while involved in 1783 with meetings of the Continental Congress, he wrote his eldest daughter, Patty, then eleven years old, to "Take care you never spell a word wrong. Always before you write a word, consider how it is spelled...It produces great praise to a lady to spell well." New Yorker James Fenimore Cooper, one of the first Americans to pen novels based on American frontier themes, was an uncertain, even unruly speller, despite his boarding school education and two years at Yale. The author of *The Last of the Mohicans* relied on his publisher to make his tales readable and regularly jumbled British and emerging American spelling conventions, using both *labor* and *labour,* and commonly writing *recive* and *secratary.*

Such orthographic misadventures at the cusp of the nineteenth century show that spelling conventions were a quite recent requirement for proper English speakers and writers, and were ignored or unknown by many. At the same time, literacy and language were becoming a preoccupation for a broad swath of Americans anxious for self-improvement. Although basic public schooling, when available, usually ended no later than age fourteen, privileged children might study grammar and other more advanced wordsmithing. Soon, ordinary Americans, from major cities and remote hamlets, were also asserting their right to aspire to the realms of higher literacy formerly reserved for elites. African-Americans, country girls, apprentices, laborers, farmers, and more were snapping up books that promised instruction in the mysteries of eloquence in speech and pen. English grammars flew out of bookshops and were passed from hand to hand. An early grammar text by Noah Webster, published in 1784 as his next step up from ABCs to literacy, was addressed to "schools of the higher class," and was patriotically "Designed for the use of English schools in AMERICA." A decade later, his and many other grammarians' offerings were eclipsed by the massive acclaim heaped on Lindley Murray's 222-page text.

Born in Pennsylvania in 1745 to Irish Quakers who became wealthy merchants in New York City, where the Murray Hill neighborhood still bears his family name, Lindley had other plans for his life, having "contracted a taste for reading for a greater degree of literary improvement." He immersed himself in the French and

Children Spelling

Scottish enlightenments and practiced law. When he and his family were tarred as Loyalists in the aftermath of the American Revolution, he left the nation of his birth for York, England and, at age fifty, published a Grammar that would take the United States by storm. Eighteen year-old Elizabeth Cooley, who tussled with Murray's text amid her domestic chores in a tiny town in Virginia's Blue Ridge Mountains, was by no means alone in finding her "Murrys (sic)...so tedious." Murray, who prefered Dr. Johnson's spellings to Webster's, would bestride grammar education until mid-century as the idea of democratic literacy was putting down deep roots in the young nation.

For grammarians and students alike, spelling was the first portal to literacy. Wrote Webster, "Orthography teaches to spell and write words with proper letters" while "Prosody teaches a true pronunciation of words." Murray went deeper, exhaustively analyzing the various sounds of each of the twenty-six letters. Students would not find some friendly "A is for apple" in Murray's grammar book. Instead, he instructs, "*A* has three sounds, the long or slender, the short or open, and the broad....*Ae* has the sound of long *E*...Some have retained this form...but others have laid it aside... Eleven pages later, his alphabetical analysis concludes by informing the student that "*Z* has the sound of an *s* uttered with a closer compression of the palate by the tongue: it is the flat *s* as in *freeze, frozen, vizier, grazier,* &c." In an 1804 ninth edition, Murray acknowledged that "A perfect alphabet of the English language and indeed every other language would contain a numbers of letters precisely equal to the simple articulate sounds belonging to the language. But this is far from being the state of the English alphabet. It has more original sounds than distinct significant letters...." In an 1808 edition, Murray peppered his spelling exercises with deliberate mistakes. One example: "It is no great merit to spel (sic) properly; but a great defect to do it incorrectly."

In a nation eager for betterment, spelling became, and still remains, an underpinning of American education, an acknowledged, though elementary, gateway to literacy. At the same time, for much of the nineteenth century, teaching spelling and learning to spell were chores that both educators and their minions suffered, but by no means in silence. As millions, including young Abraham Lincoln and legions of Elizabeth Cooleys, set their sights on the intricacies of grammar and rhetoric, mere spelling would appear to be the easiest to teach and drill, promising a clear educational path to social improvement and civic order. As a result spelling loomed large even as it was commonly regarded as child's play. Early American memoirists generally viewed spelling as an opportunity for nostalgia rather than a platform for education. Then and now, learning to spell the ever expanding English language has proved too complex to be easy, but too basic for many to take it seriously.

Well before Samuel Johnson, Noah Webster, and others created dictionaries that prescribed the conventions of orthography, spelling instruction was evoking arguments concerning the true meaning of childhood and proper ways to assess and advance children's capacities to learn. In the Anglo-American world of the late seventeenth century, philosopher John Locke, a godfather of America's eventual independence, had redefined childhood, with enduring consequences for children's education. The young, said Locke in a 1693 treatise, were not, as commonly believed, creatures steeped in original sin, but essentially blank slates upon which parents and teachers could inscribe education by mobilizing children's natural desire for praise and fear of ridicule. He prescribed a regimen of amusement rather than compulsion or salvation. By playing games with letters, he said, "*Learning* might be made a Play and Recreation to Children."

By the time of the American Revolution, even more daringly child-centric ideas about education were circulating in the new nation. Jean-Jacques Rousseau, the Swiss-born philosopher whose 1762 didactic novel *Emile, Or on Education* was especially popular in the United States, was a controversial advocate of "naturalistic" education, based on his belief that children were neither wicked nor even blank slates but had an in-born desire and ability to learn.

An even more influential Swiss thinker, Johann Heinrich Pestalozzi, became a mentor to America's educational reformers in the early nineteenth century. When he was just five his father, a surgeon and oculist, died at age thirty-three, plunging his family into debt. Puny but tireless, he grew up among women and would insist all his life that nature is a better teacher than school masters or text books, and, in his most famous work, *Leonard and Gertrude*, first published in 1781, that mothers were the best possible teachers of the young. Considered by many to be impious, if not wholly deluded, Pestalozzi tested many of his educational theories on orphans and child vagrants. This provoked widespread suspicion and alarm in many Swiss cantons in a time when serfdom and poor houses, rather than schools, were the customary lot of poor and abandoned children.

At the height of his influence in Yverdon, near Lake Geneva, Pestalozzi presided over separate boys' and girls' schools, attended by both paying students and charity cases. Students and faculty were subjected to a regime of prayer, lessons, and recreation, punctuated with austere meals. A typical day began at 5:30 in the morning and concluded at nine at night. A British educator wrote in 1908 that Pestalozzi would "have us go from experience to ideas to words, even when learning spelling." To this end, he quoted Pestalozzi's 'firm conviction...of the necessity of picture books in early childhood... talking must come before spelling...and the child is to have nothing to do with words...except in connection with things.'"

Pestalozzi was himself an uncertain speller all his life. Even his admirers would reveal that this scrawny youth "did not shine. His teachers...saw no promise in a pupil who could not spell correctly nor write legibly." Especially damning was the fact that Pestalozzi's native language, German, is virtually phonetic, compared to the many peculiarities of English. But Pestalozzi did not neglect spelling, even publishing a spelling book in 1801. An effort to engage Napoleon in his pedagogy, however, prompted from the Emperor a curt refusal to "trouble about his ABC." Pestalozzi died in 1827 at eighty-one, outliving many skeptics and attracting passionate advocates to his pedagogy, first in Prussia, where a state school system had been established in 1819, and soon in the United States.

Distinguished Americans made pilgrimages to his school and traveled to Prussia, where they encountered the fullest expression of Pestalozzi's kinder, gentler theories of childhood education. In 1836, the state of Ohio sent Cincinnati's Calvin Stowe on the grand Pestalozzian tour; three years later Alexander Dallas Bache, a great-grandson of Benjamin Franklin and president of Philadelphia's Girard College for Orphans, spent more than two years in Europe studying educational practices. In a 666-page report published in 1839, Bache wrote approvingly of a Zurich school where "The Pestalozzian lessons...are made the basis of writing, and with good success. The lowest class is taught to speak correctly, and to spell by the phonic method, to divide words into syllables and thus to count". He added "I never saw more intelligence and readiness displayed by children than in all these exercises; it affords a strong contrast to the dulness (sic) in which it is taught mechanically."

Later still, Horace Mann combined his second honeymoon with a professional visit to Europe which prominently included the schools of Prussia. He and his bride, Mary Peabody, found that even rural teachers there were well-trained and they marveled that "children of six years old often write extremely well..." Still contemptuous of Webster's spellers, Mann used his seventh annual report to colleagues and political allies to praise the Pestalozzi-inflected Prussian school system.

Pestalozzi's influence has persisted into the twentieth century and beyond. In *The School and Society*, a 1915 prescription for modern schooling, John Dewey and his wife, Evelyn, hailed Pestalozzi as an educator who had spent his life struggling to expel "from schools reliance on memorized words..." Because current ideas of child empowerment and self-esteem are rife, though still controversial in some circles, it is tempting to assume that Pestalozzi's believers, including Mann and his circle, easily prevailed in the years before the Civil War. In fact, child-centered learning remained controversial and taxpayer-funded general education even more so. Young learners were regularly exposed to boredom and fear in make-shift classrooms that were packed with "scholars" of all ages but lacked basic educational resources. So-called "soft-line" educators might curry student favor with praise and prizes, but rote recitation and whippings, or the threat of same, remained a central component of many teachers' tool kits. Schooling, at a time when most Americans lived in rural communities, tended to be nasty, brutish, and short, offering a few winter and summer weeks of non-compulsory instruction. On this schedule, it could take "abcedarians," some as young as two and others much older, a year or more to master the alphabet and begin to memorize the nonsense monosyllables commonly called the "abs" that were meant to instill proper pronunciation and accurate spelling.

Not until 1852 did bellwether Massachusetts require children aged eight to fourteen to attend school for twelve weeks a year, just six of those weeks to be consecutive. Actual attendance remained spotty.

Many who survived such educations were happy to poke fun at the process while highlighting their own accomplishments. Born in 1777, Roger B. Taney, second son of a successful Maryland tobacco planter, was already eight when he began his education, walking a six-mile roundtrip when the weather was favorable to join thirty other boys and girls in a drafty log schoolhouse. This future Chief Justice of the U.S. Supreme Court recalled his teacher as a "well-disposed but ignorant old man" who educated his charges with a copy of recently deceased British Parson Thomas Dilworth's speller, and a Bible embellished with "wretched woodcuts." These two books, said Taney, were likely "the only books our teacher had ever read."

His experience as a child of the tidewater aristocracy was by no means unique. Public schooling lagged in much of the nation. Although the Northwest Ordinance of 1787 had ordained the provision of schoolhouses, even in those regions implementation was spotty. While some states, notably Michigan and Massachusetts, pioneered publicly-financed schooling, instruction remained highly variable, due to local economic conditions and distances between population centers that required many teachers to become circuit riders. Colonial patterns persisted into the Revolution and often well beyond. Although North Carolina took schooling seriously, most Southern states tended to slight public education. They were not alone; for years the state of Rhode Island denied funds to townships seeking schooling for their children.

Even so, by 1830, public elementary schools were available to virtually all white children in the Northern states, although attendance remained voluntary and schools were grudgingly funded. Educational uniformity arose less from county or state government intervention than they were spurred by the "popularity of certain textbooks," among them Noah Webster's spellers.

Schools both public and private sought cut-rate ways to teach

young children, in part by mobilizing the perceived in-born capacities of the nation's women. Promoted by Catharine Beecher
among others, this bold extension of "republican motherhood," with
overtones of Pestalozzian benevolence, proved to be an opportunity
for women and a bargain for the nation's burgeoning classrooms.
As Beecher would say in 1846, "The mind of a young child is like
a curious instrument, capable of exquisite harmony when touched
by a skillful hand, but sending forth only annoying harshness when
unskilled..." Soon most of those skillful hands would be women's.

It had not always been so. At a 1789 town meeting in Plymouth,
Massachusetts, a foe of higher education for girls prophesied a lethal
blow to patriarchy, should "wives and daughters...look over the
shoulders of their husbands and fathers and offer to correct...such
errors in spelling as they might commit." Fifty years later, this ostensibly feminine talent was welcomed for keeping children occupied
and the price of education low. In 1800, men, some of them recent
college-educated strivers like Noah Webster and Horace Mann, or
others who were not especially bright or vigorous, like Justice Taney's
first teacher, dominated elementary education by a margin of nine
men for each woman instructor. By 1840, elementary education
had been thoroughly "feminized" and sixty years on, virtually all
elementary level teachers were women.

Teachers' wages were notoriously poor, but women's pay was
stingier yet: generally half-price or less. In villages and small towns,
most male and female instructors boarded with local officials or
parents, easing money concerns but assuring community-wide
scrutiny and moral judgment. Townspeople worried that young
women would be unable to control burly adolescent boys in one-
room schools, although this was equally likely to be a challenge for
young men trying to assert their authority in crowded classrooms.
Whole neighborhoods would gossip about girl teachers who were too
pretty, too well-dressed, too assertive. At the same time, the "spinster
teacher" who overstayed her welcome by somehow failing to get
married (and most likely denied a job anyway) or the elderly "dame"

who eked out her "widow's mite" by teaching pre-schoolers their "abs," were perennial figures of pity and fun. Excellent spelling was deemed a particularly feminine skill that was expected but hardly respected. Discoursing in 1845 on the "Beau Ideal of the Perfect Teacher" at an educational conference in Hartford, Yale astronomer and common schools advocate Denison Olmsted declared, "It is not necessary that the schoolmistress, who teaches *merely* spelling and reading, should be profound in geometry...but she must herself be an accurate speller and a good reader, and well acquainted with the rules for spelling and reading." Despite low pay, cheap sneers, and supercilious male supervision, elementary teachers who could instill spelling as a key to literacy were in great demand. Elementary teaching, once an educated man's last resort, soon became an educated woman's best opportunity. By 1850, one in four native-born women had spent some portion of her adult life teaching.

During much of the nineteenth century, the spelling experience, in all its terror, boredom, and nostalgia, dominated the remembrances of schoolmasters, schoolmarms, and pupils alike. It is no accident that the "Three R's," for "readin', 'ritin', and 'rithmatic," was a jocular phrase dating back to the 1820s, that was then, and still remains misspelled. In 1833, New England minister and memoirist Warren Burton was already bemoaning spelling education as too "tedious" to describe. Born in 1800 in Wilton, New Hampshire, Burton became a Unitarian minister in Salem, Massachusetts, befriended Nathaniel Hawthorne, and spent time at Brook Farm, the controversial and ultimately ill-fated progressive community in West Roxbury, Massachusetts. His memoir, *The District School As It Was, By One Who Went to It*, had a lot to say about spelling, little of it complimentary.

In the summer of 1804, young Warren became an "abecedarian" under the kindly tutelage of seventeen-year-old Mary Smith, an early exemplar of all the poorly-paid young women yet to come who served as combination baby-sitters and alphabet instructors. In a twenty by ten-foot schoolhouse, with a raised desk for teacher, long backless benches, and a fireplace, Miss Smith was soon instructing three-year-olds, using Scottish professor William Perry's *The Only Sure Guide to the English Tongue*, a formidable British rival to Noah Webster's home-grown spellers. Wrote Burton, "I was going to describe [Perry's text] in detail; but on second thought I forbear, for fear the description might be as tedious to my readers as the study of them was to me."

Winter school was taught by a male teacher who made Burton and his forty classmates, most of them older, recite their "abs" four times a day, while the instructor apparently focused on his own scholarship in hopes of soon escaping the low-paid monotony of elementary education. When Burton's beloved Mary left to marry a Connecticut man, the lad survived summer lessons with Mehitabel Holt, an unpleasant older teaching "Dame" whose main goal was to keep children still and quiet. As he got older, Warren also endured masters who punished bad children by having them hold heavy books at arm's-length or making them sit on the warmest or coldest benches. Some teachers favored humiliation, placing boys in girls' seats and vice versa. Burton defined the traditional long rows of most speller texts as "perpendicular reading" interspersed with "abstract moral sentences."

Even so, spelling was apparently more popular than some other subjects because spelling contests often eased the boredom of pupil and teacher alike and provided chances for children to show off and even win a few pennies. Said Burton of these rudimentary spelling bees, "The child cares no more in his heart about the arrangement of vowels and consonants...than he does how many chips lie...in the school-house wood-pile. But he does care whether he is at the head or foot of his class; whether the money dangles from his own neck or of another's. This is the secret of the interest in spelling."

Burton observed that "Girls are more likely to arrive at and keep the first place in the class," adding "I believe that they generally have a memory more fitted for catching and holding words and other signs addressed to the eye than the other sex." An exception was a classmate whom Burton dubbed "Memorus Wordus," a reading and spelling "machine" who knew his letters but not always their meanings. Told by his teacher to "spell" Jonas, an older and duller boy who had been sent to cut wood for the school house stove, "Memorus" instead administered a list of spelling words to the irked arborist. Reworked and elaborated over many years by Burton and other educators, this tale was almost certainly too "tall" and too "cute" to be strictly true.

By age ten, Warren was done with summer school – chores awaited boys his age in what was still a predominantly agricultural community — and by age thirteen his days in District School were over. He prepared himself, likely aided by a tutor, to attend Harvard College, and taught school briefly before enrolling at the Harvard Divinity School where he was ordained in 1828.

If turn-of-the-century literacy education, as portrayed by Burton, seemed mainly to foster boredom and fear, by the 1830s New England in particular was ablaze with more radical notions, spearheaded by Horace Mann and lesser-known figures including Bronson Alcott. Most likely remembered for fathering Louisa May Alcott, the beloved author of *Little Women* and *Little Men*, he was born in rural Connecticut in 1799. For more than eighty years, wrote a 1937 biographer, "he remembered how he had practised [sic] his A,B, C's, laboriously conned out of Noah Webster's Spelling Book, with chalk, upon his mother's parlor floor" whereby he soon also discovered that his mother "did not always spell her words in quite the way approved by Noah Webster." Alcott's rather informal education began at age six and ended at thirteen which, said his biographer, "was no worse than schools elsewhere in Connecticut, and was rather better than those of most other states." Alcott and his cousins "learned to read and write and spell by processes ingeniously devised to produce the least possible reward for the greatest expenditure of effort."

Expected to support his family, young Bronson spent several seasons as a Yankee peddler of goods and trinkets, mainly in Virginia and South Carolina, but he regularly returned home owing more than he had earned. What he was sure he could, nay, must do, was to become a schoolmaster. For Alcott, teaching would not be a steppingstone to a more lucrative and manly profession but his life's goal. He was a voracious if disorganized reader who admired Locke and Pestalozzi and attempted like them to emulate an ideal mother. He was surely pleased in his declining years when some hailed him as the "Pestalozzi of America."

Alcott embodied a spirit of transcendental innovation that would madden more conservative educators both inside and beyond New England. Refusing to view children as "limbs of Satan" or even as Lockean blank slates, he had his own ideas about the moral and intellectual culture of children and regularly used his own meager resources (depriving his growing family in the process) to promote gymnastics and vegetarianism, hold parent conferences, and equip his classrooms with art objects while also providing his pupils their own individual desks, texts, and writing slates, a benefit almost unheard of at that time.

Spelling instruction was a central and time-consuming component of Alcott's inventive but peculiar pedagogy. Each morning at nine, in a school housed in an ornate former Boston Masonic Temple, older students were expected to work silently for an hour "at their desks, engaged in writing their journals or practicing spelling lessons." Meanwhile Alcott would assemble the seven youngest students who "cannot use a dictionary very intelligently," to listen while he spelled and defined some words. Then older pupils were tested on thirty spelling words. Finally each word was "taken up one by one, and not merely defined but illustrations of all their meanings, literal and imaginative, were given either by original or remembered sentences" while Alcott interjected from time to time with "disquisitions" on sundry topics. Alcott's school failed in 1836 after just two years, a victim of its schoolmaster's over-spending and his penchant for religious controversy. Even Unitarians, it seems, would not suffer spelling lessons to which Alcott invited a black child. Worse yet, some of Alcott's lessons were interspersed with vague, but not vague enough, disquisitions that came very close to informing young scholars where babies came from. By the end, just three children remained.

If Webster's and most other spellers offered "perpendicular reading" and rote, the spellers of another minister, William Holmes McGuffey energized at least some students struggling with the English language. Wrote prairie author Hamlin Garland, "I wish to acknowledge my deep obligation to Professor McGuffey, whoever he may have been" for saving his youthful self from the "vulgarity and baseness" of schoolhouse back benches where bored older boys chewed, cussed, slouched, and mocked their teachers and classmates. For Garland, who grew up in 1870s South Dakota and Iowa before lighting out for the literary territories of Boston and New York, the "bleak little shack at the corner of our farm" that passed for a winter school was a portal to success where he had lyrical memories of "trotting away across the plain to spelling schools" and competing in local "spell downs."

McGuffey's own early education relied on the Bible, augmented by its nearest modern competitor, Webster's *Blue-Back Speller*, effectively the only American speller available in the west in early years. By the time he was fourteen, William had been recruited to teach forty-eight children in Calcutta, Ohio at a rather generous two dollars per head for the term. Like Webster and so many other promising but struggling young men, he was finding his way from lowly elementary teaching to the higher realms available to men equipped with learning, Latin, and oratory. McGuffey's graded readers were popular with teachers in one-room schoolhouses who, busy with beginners, struggled to spare older students, like Hamlin Garland, from utter boredom.

McGuffey and his younger brother Alexander focused on uplift and patriotic inspiration, but also added "spell and define" exercises that highlighted lists of common spelling errors. By 1879, the McGuffey heirs had published a revised *Eclectic Spelling-Book*, reworked the diacritical marks that Noah Webster had invented more than fifty years earlier, and dubbed "the latest edition of *Webster's Unabridged Dictionary*" their official source for "orthography, pronunciation, and syllabication [sic]." Packed with words both ordinary and exotic, this speller's 144 pages included batches of "words which require Care in Spelling," such as *scholar, autumn, ninny,* and *diligent.* The object "has been not to appeal merely to arbitrary memory" but to "aid the pupil in acquiring knowledge of our language."

Industrialist Henry Ford, born in 1863, would attribute much of his later success to his battered 1857 version of the *McGuffey Reader.* In 1933, he relocated an old McGuffey family house from Ohio to Greenfield Village, his Dearborn, Michigan memorial to his own upbringing and achievements. Three years later, Ford, along with twelve other notables, including Hamlin Garland, spearheaded a McGuffey Centenary celebration, that included a centenary book of the McGuffey canon that included, from the First Reader, "Mary's Lamb" and "The Little Star" that twinkles yet for the children of today).

Ford was no scholar, and spelling errors pepper the blizzard of notes, jotting, and comments, inscribed in pencil or pen, on cardboard, telegraph pads, envelopes, scraps of pink or yellow paper, all of which have been faithfully preserved by the museum that bears his name. As the Great War threatened to involve the U.S., he laid plans for his 1915 "Pease" Ship and railed against "natians" and warmongers seeking to "get Ritch." But he showed great regard for language, consulting with experts on Greek and Latin roots, and making lists of words, apparently for his own continuing self-improvement. Unlike industrialist Andrew Carnegie, who was a generation older and a keen spelling simplifier, Ford pursued correctness. In a note penciled when he was already famous, he wrote, "Could read all of the [McGuffey] First Reader when I started school [at age eight]. My mother taught me."

For some time after the Civil War, spelling education seemed still to be in thrall to the twin eminences of Webster and McGuffey, intensifying nostalgia for the fading one-room schoolhouse and its presumed product, the eager, respectful, and well-drilled pupil. The spelling experience seems almost embalmed, in part because it so regularly shows up as a coming-of-age touchstone in the childhood reminiscences of such writers as Garland and his near-contemporary, Laura Ingalls Wilder. In her 1937 tale of prairie life, *On the Banks of Plum Creek*, "Ma" gives her girls a speller she has been saving among her most prized possessions. "But Laura looked at Ma's book and shook her head. She could not read. She was not even sure of all the letters."

In 1871, thirty-three-year-old Indiana native Edward Eggleston published *The Hoosier-Schoolmaster: A Story of Backwoods Life in Indiana*. His immensely popular novel, set in the 1850s, resuscitated the popularity of spelling bees and was an early example of the American dialect novel, a genre that both celebrated and poked fun at regional vernacular and countrified speech and spelling patterns. In the years after the Civil War, such dialect sketches and novels were also employed by more famous authors, including Mark Twain, Bret Harte, and Joel Chandler Harris. By emphasizing the separation of high and low culture, and contrasting the "standard" speech of well-educated natives to those of hayseeds, immigrants, and African-Americans, this dialect craze at the very least cast doubt on Noah Webster's vision of a unitary American language characterized by consistency in pronunciation, word use, and spelling across the nation.

Ralph Hartsook is Eggleston's hero school-master and much of the plot is propelled by young Ralph's assigned role as Hoopole County, Indiana's authority on all things academic, spelling foremost. His rural constituency places little value on actual reading and writing, says Eggleston, but they seem "impressed with the difficulties of English orthography, and there is a solemn conviction that the chief end of man is to learn to spell. ' Know Webster's Elementary' came down from Heaven..."

Hartsook's trial by Webster arrives early in his tenure in the form of a spell-down. Out-spelling the schoolmaster is the overt goal; pairing the promising young teacher with a pretty girl from a leading local family is an unstated objective. Ralph's first serious spell-down contender is Jim Phillips, a "tall, lank, stoop-shouldered fellow who had never distinguished himself in any other pursuit than spelling" and knew "a heap of spelling-book." For a half hour, Hartsook and Phillips battle to a tie, leading our narrator to exclaim, "What a blessed thing our crooked orthography is! Without it, there could be no more spelling [contests]."

Ralph outlasts Jim, and it seems that the school-master will prevail. But what novelist would wish an outcome so dreary and obvious? Instead, Hannah Thomson, a teenaged "bound girl" who drudges for the wife of a local worthy, rises to the occasion in a dress of cheap blue calico. Ralph is instantly smitten by this shy and mistreated young woman. As he stumbles, she astounds everyone by easily spelling "daguerreotype." (Spoiler alert: by the end of the novel, Ralph and Hannah are married. Such is the power of superior spelling!)

Less romantic but firmly situated in the seemingly eternal tedium of nineteenth century spelling lore was the real-life experience of Vermonter Lucia B. Downing, a tall fourteen-year-old who in August, 1882 launched a teaching career in a long abandoned rural red schoolhouse. Entrusted with just four "scholars," all members of the same family, and an older girl who seemed virtually unable read the "little purple primer" that she nevertheless carried at all times, Lucia struggled to fill her ten-week school term. In a reminiscence published six years after her death in 1945 she wrote "when each pupil had read and cipherered and spelled and passed the water and recessed and recessed and passed the water and spelled and had a lesson in geography and read and spelled, there was usually an hour before I dared dismiss them." Nor had she dared ask about her salary. She was elated at term's end to receive $3.50 a week, of which two dollars were in cash and the remainder in-kind room and board with a wealthy farm family, "which, I may say, was a most generous arrangement…" Fifteen students showed up for Lucia's second term. By 1889 she had graduated Phi Beta Kappa from the University of Vermont and taught until her marriage.

Downing's little red school house notwithstanding, spelling education was beginning to change quite dramatically. Launched in the 1880s, the Teachers College at Columbia University in New York City raised the profile of schools of education across much of the nation by encouraging research as well as teacher training. Progressivist ideas began trickling into the hidebound spelling curriculum. As waves of non-English- speaking immigrants landed on U.S. shores, and white-collar and managerial jobs multiplied in the corporate American economy, critics and experts endeavored to apply science, statistics, and new techniques to usher in a Golden Age of spelling inquiry.

Spelling 'R' Not Us in Nebraska

An early reformer was Joseph Mayer Rice, a Philadelphia physician who gave up medicine in his thirties to become spelling education's first "muckraker." Inveighing against what he called "The Futility of the Spelling Grind," Rice undertook to put elementary education "on a scientific basis." In a 1907 series of reports published in *Forum*, a progressive monthly founded by his older brother Isaac, Rice laid out a sweeping prescription for healthy spelling, saying "The traditional standard in spelling is perfection; but this standard is unreasonable, and cannot be too soon abandoned."

Rice, a son of German-Jewish immigrants, had spent two years in Germany studying education practices. In 1892 he embarked on a six-month examination of thirty-six of America's public school systems. His resulting book revealed much inept and mechanical teaching, with spelling instruction arguably the most wretched of all. Said Rice in his preface, "much can be learned of the School System of any city during fifteen minutes spent in the ABC class of almost any school visited at random." He scrapped early data culled from twenty school districts because he suspected that teachers were over-enunciating his list of fifty vocabulary words to help their students spell better than they would ordinarily – clearly an early instance of "teaching to the test."

His report on a spelling class in Buffalo, New York was especially scathing and merits an extended description:

> The teacher informed me that it was to be a new lesson, and that I should therefore have the oppor-tunity to learn her method of teaching spelling.... When the little ones were ready, they began to spell in concert, and continued doing so until the list of words on that page was completed. Each word was spelled twice...and in a sing-song...When the children had sung all the words in the list, they were told to spell them once more....I expected to hear another subject announced, but I learned to my utter amazement, that the pupils were to be treated to a third course. "We will now write the

words." ...When all was quiet, one of the pupils called out, "I ain't got no ruler." In answer to this the teacher, without correcting or even paying the slightest attention to the incorrect language that had been used by the child, said to him: "You don't need a ruler. Do it the way you *done* it yesterday." Then the words of the oft-repeated list were slowly dictated by the teacher. When the word "steal" was reached, she remarked, "Spell the 'steal' you spelled this morning, not the 'steel' you spelled yesterday."

Rice ardently advocated a new spelling regimen in which fewer but more practical and commonly-used words would be studied a few minutes a day, instead of the forty or fifty-minute chunks that were the norm. He believed that only maturity, not dull repetition, could ultimately solve the problem of careless or defective orthography. Said Rice, "the wise teacher will acquaint herself with as many methods and devices as possible, and change from one to the other, in order to relieve the tedium..." adding, "under no circumstances should more than fifteen minutes daily be devoted to the subject." Essentially optimistic about the ultimate survival of standard spelling, he found minimal differences in spelling prowess between a large eastern school and a smaller western one. He also saw no significant disparity based on class or ethnicity, saying that poor and immigrant children spelled no worse, and sometimes better, than the middle-class and native-born. Rice died in 1934 but was invoked as recently as 1999 in a newspaper article exploring the use, abuse, and value of homework, especially in the elementary and middle school years.

In the new century, others followed Rice in questioning the legacy of Websterian modes of spelling and reading education.

Attempts during the Progressive era to make spelling education more scientific and helpful reached new heights in the 19-teens. In 1913 Henry Suzzallo, who had briefly taught at Columbia, published

The Teaching of Spelling: A Critical Study of Recent Tendencies in Method. Just two years later, Suzzallo, the California-born son of Czech immigrants and himself a former elementary school principal, became the innovative, beloved, yet controversial president of the University of Washington. His firing in 1926 by Governor Roland H. Hartley raised national issues of educational funding and state labor practices. At his death in 1933 at age fifty-eight, Suzzallo was head of the Carnegie Foundation to Advance Teaching, surely making him the highest-ranking educator ever to write a monograph on spelling pedagogy.

In the introduction, a colleague in elementary education laid out Suzzallo's challenge. "To the large majority of teachers – even of those who are progressive – spelling is a hopeless subject," wrote Frank M. McMurry. The nation's newspapers, he observed, regularly shook their collective heads over bad spelling and were fixated on mechanical drills, even though these were "one of the clumsiest tools we have in the field of education."

Suzzallo's critique began with a sympathetic nod to the ambitions and fears of spelling instructors. "Next to the complete inability to read, poor spelling is to the public the surest sign that one is not educated....The lay critic...readily thinks that the children of his own generation were better taught; he then lays the lash of odious comparison upon the teachers of his own children." Despite a quarter century of significant improvement, added Suzzallo, spelling teachers remain terrified, not least because of the confusing and unruly multiplication of teaching methods, new and old, that made it difficult "for the old teacher, much more for the young teacher, to steer himself." (Of course, "herselves" bore the brunt of this spelling rollercoaster.) Like Rice, and many others, Suzzallo objected to spelling books and teaching regimens that imposed adult standards and dictionary words rather than age-appropriate vocabulary actually used in school and at home. Spelling, he indicated, worked best not as an independent and intensive course of study, but rather as a vital tool alongside all the other school subjects.

Suzzallo also doubted the usefulness and "great popularity" of oral spelling fests including those nineteenth century spelling sweeteners, soon to become a twentieth-century fixture: the spell-down, spelling match, or spelling bee. He called them "naturally artificial." In the long-running and inevitable struggle between the ear and the eye, he came down firmly in favor of the written word. Phonetics, he said, could help students with correct letter sounds and some word meanings, but would prove useless to the challenges of diphthongs and silent letters. Oral spelling, he added, was an unsatisfactory substitute for teaching real spelling competency. The spelling match failed, he said, by emphasizing individual letters, rather than words that could last a lifetime. As nineteenth century oratorical traditions gave way to twentieth century mass media, the ability to spell out loud seemed to be more a flashy talent than a necessity for broader literacy among the rising white-collar, managerial, and professional classes. Instead, new era orthographers turned their attention to selecting and compiling lists of words considered most frequent, most useful, or "demon words" that were commonly used but devilishly difficult to spell.

Enthusiasm for such spelling lists was fueled by a conviction that expertise and quantification could create a spelling science. Leading the way were university educators and specialists affiliated with emerging "think tanks" including Carnegie's Foundation and the Russell Sage Foundation. To this day, no one has solved the dilemma of the Vice president who could not spell "potato" in a New Jersey class in 1992.

3 | Spelling Freedom

Seething in Philadelphia's summer heat, the Continental Congress in July, 1776 proclaimed American independence and the birth of the United States. Less noted in that momentous year, a sixty-three year old Philadelphia educator was preparing his first edition of a spelling book that would be revolutionary in its own right. Preceding Noah Webster's speller by seven years, Anthony Benezet's *Pennsylvania Spelling-Book or Youth's Friendly Instructor and Monitor* did more than teach children ABCs and moral lessons. In this year claiming that "all men are created equal," Benezet actually insisted that could be so.

His speller, described as an "easy Plan, for exciting the attention...of Children..." was the fruition of a life devoted to education and imbued with his strong dislike of harsh classroom discipline. As Benezet soon explained his "Friendly Instructor" was meant for every boy and girl, including "illiterate Domesticks" and "the meanest Servant" who would thereby achieve "eternal happiness" along with social usefulness. "Particular care," he wrote, "should be taken to make children spell correctly..." His speller concludes with an attack on the "cheapness" and "absurd thrift" of communities disinclined to establish schools and adequately pay teachers.

Born in 1713 to Huguenot parents, Benezet experienced religious persecution in France, Holland, and England before settling in Philadelphia, where he became a Quaker in 1731 and soon a friend of Benjamin Franklin. A small man of frail constitution but dogged energy, Benezet was an early and ardent opponent of slavery. He and his wife, Joyce Marriott, herself a Quaker minister, became conscience vegetarians, protesting both animal cruelty and African enslavement in an era when few had difficulty benefiting from chattel slavery, and most had no trouble at all eating meat. Already known in his adopted town for fostering female education, Benezet in 1750 began his longest and proudest educational initiative: schooling, often in his own home, African-American boys and girls. The prevailing notion that blacks were educationally inferior, he said, was "a vulgar prejudice, founded on the pride or ignorance" of slave masters. With like-minded Quaker colleagues Anthony Benezet would work to further the education of black students until and beyond his death in May, 1784 when he left a portion of his estate to continue the education of young black Philadelphians. What he could not know, of course, was that his initiative would for decades mark a high point in the nation's efforts to educate slaves, emancipated slaves, or even African-American free boys and girls. Even Massachusetts' Horace Mann, the national champion of common schooling, was too timid to take sides in 1845 when Boston officials consigned black students to the "run-down and neglected" Smith Grammar School. Fearing funding setbacks, Mann even ignored a scolding from abolitionist leader William Lloyd Garrison. Yet, as he headed to Washington in 1848 to take up a seat in Congress, Mann delivered a final schools report that boasted that Massachusetts' school system knew "no distinction of rich and poor, of bond and free..." Four years later, while preparing to become the first president of Ohio's Antioch College, he would tell a black audience that "in intellect, blacks are inferior to the whites, while in sentiment and affections, the whites are inferior to the blacks." Antioch would soon open its doors to a few women, but, despite its radical reputation, the college struggled for years to achieve a modicum of racial integration.

As childhood education began to take hold in America, very few free African-American children and almost none who were enslaved, were allowed to attend school. By the 1830s, even as public schooling dramatically expanded in northern, mid-western, and some southern states, opportunities for black children and adults waned. As abolitionism made gains in Britain and parts of the United States, slave-holding states felt ever more embattled. When Virginia slave preacher Nat Turner led a bloody uprising in August 1831, most southern and border states that had not already done so rushed to outlaw education for slaves and often banned free people of color as well. Efforts to teach spelling and other language skills to African-Americans became "unlawful assemblies" as legislators imposed harsh fines, whipping, and other punishments for those men and women, black or white, with the temerity to educate them. In the North even emancipated African-Americans could not be assured the means of basic literacy. Cincinnati, a bastion of public education, barred black children; in New York, city schools were clearly unequal. However, Quaker heirs to the ethics of Anthony Benezet encouraged and facilitated schools in Philadelphia, most of them run by African-Americans themselves.

Lawmaking, of course, rarely, if ever, achieves total compliance. In slave states before the Civil War significant numbers of African-Americans, sometimes aided by sympathetic whites, found ways to instill forbidden literacy. Learners of all ages flocked to "clandestine" schools, gathering in swamps and canebreaks; sharing tattered spelling books in the dark of night, or pretending to learn only racially "appropriate" skills such as laundering, shoemaking, or blacksmithing rather than the forbidden ABCs. Some Pastors would turn their

Sunday services and sermons into secret reading instruction sessions. The number of slaves rescued by Harriet Tubman's Underground Railroad pales by comparison to the number of children and adults who got at least a taste of reading and writing in underground schools.

Modern scholars have documented ways in which slaves, as well as freed persons, and some poor Southern whites, found clever ways to decode the coveted secrets of language despite whippings or even worse. It is safe to say, though, that stealth, cleverness, and tenacity were the most successful tools of literacy. In one case titled "Slave Testimony: 'We Slipped and Learned to Read'" twenty-one year old Thomas Johnson, a bright and determined but unlettered slave in a Richmond tobacco factory, found a way to make his master's young son into his personal spelling coach. Armed with a speller that he could not yet parse, Johnson would later explain that he would challenge the young master to spell words that the slave Thomas had not yet achieved, exclaiming "lor's over me, you can spell nice" as he slipped away to commit his newly-acquired words to memory. Even a harsh warning when another Richmond slave was caught forging papers proved to be an incentive. Johnson became a preacher and missionary who liked to happily remind his flock how he had bamboozled both master and the master's son by illegally learning to spell and read.

The most famous illicit reader before the Civil War was Frederick Douglass, the abolitionist orator, advisor to President Lincoln, and statesman. In his several autobiographies, the acquisition of literacy is a central and powerful theme. Born into slavery circa 1817 in Maryland, Douglass was introduced to literacy by his naïve mistress, Sophia, whose domineering husband, Hugh Auld, soon squelched her illegal activity. Once he was sent from the rural plantation to toil in a bustling Baltimore shipyard, Douglass managed to decode the letters "L," "S," "F," and "A" (for larboard, starboard, forward, and aft). Trading bread for "the bread of knowledge," Douglass also cajoled working class white youths into helping him acquire the rest of the alphabet. His copy-book was, he said, a "board fence, brick wall, and pavement; my pen and ink was a lump of chalk....I then... continued copying the Italics in Webster's Spelling Book, until I could make them all without looking on [sic] the book."

Frederick Douglass and Son

By 1833, five years before he would make a successful break for freedom, Douglass would sometimes slip into a Sabbath school in Baltimore that openly taught free African-American children, but

"having learned to read and write already, I was more of a teacher...."
Forced to return to the rural Eastern Shore, he forged a brief alliance
with "Wilson," an idealistic young white man, to create a school
for black children. Within days, a local mob rushed in to close the
school, during which "One of this pious crew told me that...I wanted
to be another Nat Turner." Douglass continued to find ways to
teach, at times under threat, but often left alone by a more lenient
master or community. It was surprising, he wrote, "with what ease
[his students] provided themselves with spelling-books. These were
mostly the cast-off books of their young masters or mistresses." One
child's tedium, it seems, was another's treasure-trove.

As the United States hurtled towards war in the late 1850s, one
Southern senator remained optimistic about the fate of the nation,
declaring, "above all other people we are one, and above all books
which have united us in the bond of common language, I place the
good old Spelling-Book of Noah Webster." To say that Jefferson
Davis of Mississippi, soon to become the first and last President
of the Confederate States of America, was mistaken is obvious,
even if we look no further than the slave states' tenacious efforts
to deny Webster's lessons to African-American learners. Passionate
differences over the American language were as old as the British
colonies and would remain tense. Old Noah himself had been a
famously rambunctious fomenter of linguistic and orthographic
controversy. Yet however fictive it was, Webster's (and Davis's) dream
of an America unified by its common language and spelling could
apparently still offer some comfort on the brink of dissolution.

Many of the states that joined the Confederacy had banned not
only basic education for African-Americans but had also stinted on
education for middle and working-class whites. Private academies
and Female seminaries, supplemented by education in the North or
in Britain, were available mainly to the wealthy and well-connected.
White southerners of middling means generally picked schools run
by their chosen religious denomination. In sparsely populated communities parents sent their children to "old field schools," paying

what they could to hire a parade of instructors of varying ability and often brief tenure. In some states, including Georgia, publically financed programs teaching basics to poor white children were very controversial. Charleston, South Carolina also created some free schools at public expense. In North Carolina, Calvin Henderson Wiley, a lawyer, minister, and legislator, spearheaded the creation of common schools and became his state's first schools superintendent in 1853. Five years later, he founded the ambitious *North-Carolina Journal of Education* and attended a national educators' convention in Cincinnati. There he shared a stage with Horace Mann, to whom he would be favorably compared. By 1860, North Carolina schools were considered the best in the South.

Then came April 14, 1861.

Webster spellers had long sold in the South, although they were less popular there than elsewhere. But once war broke out, it became obvious to educators in the seceding states that Southern children were at the mercy of books that were printed and published in places like New York, Boston, and Cincinnati. Would-be Confederate publishers, facing federal blockades, had to scramble for paper, ink, and content. Webster's spellers were in great demand; even more so as his copyrights, annulled by war, were regularly used to keep southern white children occupied and educated. From all over the South, Confederate Primers and Spellers, often poorly printed in tiny letters and bound in cardboard covers, mushroomed. In Raleigh, Superintendent Wiley encouraged publication of an "Our Own" series of school materials, including *Our Own Spelling Book*, printed on paper harvested from North Carolina's forests. Produced in the thousands, textbooks like these dominated southern publishing during the war.

Educators in all the breakaway states soon found themselves in crisis as they dealt with constricted finances. Meanwhile, the war's huge manpower requirements could and did turn older students and their teachers into soldiers. Soon after Fort Sumter, Wiley rallied educators and other concerned North Carolinians to help him save the state's schools. Only the "enlistment of the mind and heart of all ages, of both sexes, of every class" (but not, obviously, slaves) could assure the success of the new nation aborning. Books and lessons written by and for Southerners, and expanded schooling for their children, he declared, were as vital to the Confederate cause as the war itself. Across the Confederacy, most spellers were imitative copies of Webster's or McGuffey's spellers and readers. The word "Confederate" on title pages was often the only clue to their provenance and ideology.

North Carolinian Marinda Branson Moore's 1864 *Dixie Elementary Spelling Book for the Use of Common Schools*, published in Raleigh, was priced at three dollars, a hefty sum for a very plain book of 120 small pages, bound in brown cloth, and printed on beige paperboard. Moore hailed from north-central Rockingham County and was a rarity: a married female teacher who had established her own school. Moore produced an array of primers and readers during the war. The *Dixie Speller* would be her last. A Branson family genealogy, published three decades later, hailed her piety, patriotism, literary talent, and bravery as she faced an extended illness that killed her at age thirty-five on June, 27, 1864.

But her *Dixie Speller* proved to be almost brutally frank. Death would prevent Moore from seeing the Confederacy fall, but she harbored few illusions and did not spare her young readers. "I hope we will have peace by the time I am old enough to go to war....If little boys fight, old folks whip them for it; but when men fight, they say 'how brave!'."

Slaves and former slaves did not wait for the war to end before staking out their own long-withheld right to literacy. The complementary memoirs of former slaves Jacob Stroyer and William Henry Singleton offer vivid examples. Stroyer was born in 1849 on a plantation near Columbia, South Carolina where he was one of the more than four hundred slaves owned by John and later Matthew Singleton. A slave named Henry Singleton, born some years earlier, toiled on a plantation almost as large in New Bern, North Carolina. It was owned by Spyer Singleton, who, in a common practice at the time, imposed his surname on all his slaves. There seems to have been no family connection between these two Singleton squires living in adjoining states.

Learning to read and spell was central to both men's struggles to overcome the huge obstacle of slavery and to take a rightful place in American society. Both would eventually move north and become respected ministers. Stroyer learned to read at about age thirteen but reveals little in his memoir to explain his success. In his 1879 *Sketches of My Life in the South*, young Jacob is confronted by an overseer who suspects, with good reason, that this slave is literate and warns the widowed Mrs. Singleton, "that boy can read very well now, and you know madam, it is against the law for a negro to get an education... Then mistress asked me, 'can you read, Jacob?...I answered, 'I don't know, ma'am....'" When the overseer suddenly pulled out a newspaper and demanded to know "who told you to say the words in the book," Jacob, who reflexively began reading the newspaper, saved his skin by saying, "nobody sir, I said them myself." This brave but clearly inadequate answer defused the situation, mainly because both the overseer and his mistress were certain that, "if we can manage to keep him from gaining any more education he will eventually lose what little he has..."

Plucked in 1863 from the plantation along with thousands of other slaves, and forcibly recruited into the Confederate Army, Stroyer still found opportunities to extend and deepen his literacy. In 1864, deployed in the defense of near-by Fort Sumter, this unwilling fourteen-year-old soldier "carried my spelling book with me, and although the Northerners were firing upon us I tried to keep up my study." It is hard to imagine a more ironic scene than a slave reading his Webster amid the clamor of a war whose tenets prohibited African-American education.

William Henry Singleton's path to literacy took much longer but was no less remarkable. Although he knew very early that his master's brother was actually his father, he was treated at least as badly as all the other slave children. His parentage caused a rift between the Singleton brothers, by "continually reminding them of something they wanted to forget," and was certainly exacerbated by this slave child's very light complexion. At age four, William, lured by pieces of candy, was sold to a white Atlanta widow who bought up slaves for speculative purposes. Helped by other slaves and his own tenacity, William eventually was reunited with his mother on the New Bern plantation.

This was a triumph but hardly a happy ending. One day, the master's son Edward, who was the same age as William (and his unacknowledged cousin) ordered him to carry a book bag home from school. "I slung the bag over my shoulder but did not take any of the books out. But Edward said I took one of his books out and opened it. When his father heard that...he whipped me very severely," redoubling his blows when the child continued to protest his innocence.

This experience certainly discouraged William from reading but seems to have intensified both his oral memory and desire for freedom. By 1858, he and fellow slaves were listening closely as their masters and overseers talked about the horrors of the North's social and economic system. Said William, "We only knew, of course, what we were told. We could not read or write and if any of us had tried to learn to read or write we would have been severely punished." Nevertheless, the slaves on the Singleton plantation were soon understanding plenty – whispers of Lincoln, John Brown, and the Underground Railroad – and reaching their own conclusions.

In the spring of 1862, Union troops under Gen. Ambrose E. Burnside gained control of New Bern. William quickly deserted his Confederate regiment and escaped to the Union side, making him one of many "contrabands" seeking protection behind Union lines. Elected as their Colonel by hundreds of other contrabands, he offered the black men's services to the Union Army. During the months it took to gain Union recognition, Singleton became Burnside's servant. One day in 1862, introduced as "the little fellow who got up a colored regiment," William found himself shaking hands with President Lincoln. In May of 1863, in the wake of the Emancipation Proclamation, William Henry Singleton, once the property of North Carolina's slave-owning Singletons, became a sergeant in a regiment headed by Colonel James C. Beecher, brother of Catharine Beecher and Harriet Beecher Stowe. Singleton served in South Carolina, Georgia, and Florida, sustaining a leg injury before he was honorably mustered out in 1866.

But this battle-hardened veteran was still barely able to read. Relocating in New Haven, Connecticut, he joined the A.M.E. Zion Church. "It was in that church that I learned to read, although I had learned the alphabet and how to spell simple words while I was in the Army...and read as many books as I could." Summing up in 1922 what was already a very long and fruitful life, William Henry Singleton wrote, "God has been very good to me. I have preached His Gospel. I can read His book."

As these experiences exemplify, the war stimulated an already strong desire for reading, writing, and spelling. Making their way to Union lines, freed slaves who could already read and write helped others to learn, penning letters to be delivered to loved ones, and petitioning politicians and other authorities. Despite the difficult and often demeaning chores they were assigned in the Union Army, and the threats they faced from former masters, many set up or continued schooling and, like Stroyer, kept their spelling books always near at hand. By war's end, thousands of freedmen and women were pursuing literacy so long denied. In 1866, some 600,000 copies of Noah Webster's *Blue-Back Speller*, for most white northerners by now a quaint bit of nostalgia, were purchased by former slaves seeking to unlock a freer and richer life. This speller became a talisman because it was small and easy to carry (or hide, if need be) and, unlike remaining Confederate spellers, could be deemed trustworthy.

One woman of sixty, "just beginning to spell," was so enrapt with learning that she "spells her lessons all the evening, then she dreams about it, and wakes up thinking about it," according to a northern teacher working with some of the newly liberated.

Almost sixty years later, during the Great Depression, the Federal Writers' Project fanned out across the South collecting stories of African-Americans who had once been slaves. Experiences, most often joyful, of learning to spell, read, and write were seared into the recollections of scores of elderly former slaves. Their stories were replete with struggles and proud moments; slave owners who ignored anti-literacy laws, and those who punished their slaves for any hint of learning.

Ninety-year-old South Carolinian "Unca" Jimmie Johnson had nothing but good feelings for the "Old Missus" who taught him the alphabet and "Masser" who "let me take my Webster's blue back speller and my history with me when I would drive with him... Sometimes on our drives masser would tell me some Latin words, but I never did study Latin – just English." Likewise, Mary Annagady, born in North Carolina in 1857, credited her mistress Bettie and Bettie's daughter Sallie for teaching "my A B C's ... When I learned to Spell B-a-k-e-r, Baker, I thought that was something. The next word I felt proud to spell was s-h-a-d-y, shady, the next l-a-d-y, lady. I would spell them out loud as I picked up chips in the yard to build a fire with. My missuss Bettie gave me a blue back spelling book." Aleck Trimble attended a school in tiny Shiloh in East Texas run by Mrs. Tunsten, a white woman who taught whites and blacks together, although Trimble recalled that she sent her own children elsewhere. "I t'ought she was a good teacher," he said, "but she whip me half a day one time 'cause I didn't spell 'gangrene.' She whip me 'till I learn how to spell it and I ain't neber forgit." .

Such hindsight, both rueful and triumphant, adds depth and perspective to the lives of survivors and their kin, but, among a general audience may also encourage a veneer of nostalgia and in-evitability. During and after the Civil War, achieving literacy, with or without the promise of all those copies of Webster, would prove rewarding, but remained costly, difficult, and dangerous as well. As early as 1862, when the Union Navy occupied the Sea Islands of South Carolina, college students and teachers, many from the most prestigious Northern schools, flooded in to educate some ten thousand slaves whose masters had fled to the Confederate mainland. Eager and committed, these "warriors" for education, dubbed "Gideonites," were also often naïve and paternalistic. Generally unaware of African-Americans' years of clandestine efforts to gain education, they were surprised to find two black-run schools already in operation. Gideonite experiments with literacy education – a key aspect of what historians have dubbed America's "rehearsal for Reconstruction"— prefigured brief but important post-war educational efforts led by the Freedmen's Bureau, and augmented by Northern-based religious and charitable organizations.

By the fall of 1865, school rooms were being prepared for floods of students. Many were children, of course, but large numbers of their elders also took part. While public education for white southerners still lagged much of the rejoined nation, African-American groups in Georgia, North Carolina, and elsewhere would raise a million dollars by 1870 to build common schools. Despite that hard-earned triumph, black teachers and their communities regularly faced white southern hostility and northern condescension, which is not to deny that a huge literacy gap indeed faced millions of former slaves.

While many former slaves made do with battered Webster spellers and saved them into their old age, new books became available for this emerging cohort of learners. Two of the most successful were Lydia Maria Child's 1865 The *Freedmen's Book*, which she subsidized so that her 277- page book could sell for sixty cents. Her competition came mainly from the evangelical American Tract Society of Boston, whose widely circulated 160-page *The Freedman's Spelling Book* sold for thirty cents. Both of these texts went beyond spelling and reading lessons to instruct, inspire, and admonish a freed people.

Child, born in 1802 in Massachusetts, was the most successful female journalist of her time, bolstering her family's finances while producing political essays, novels, and poems, including "A Boy's Thanksgiving Day," now much better known as "Over the River and Through the Woods." An early advocate for women's and Native American rights, she soon turned her attention to slavery and emancipation. Before the war, Child was already a trusted ally of William Lloyd Garrison and an ardent admirer of John Brown. Even more radically, she advocated black suffrage, land grants for former slaves, and even racial intermarriage as a way to bind up the deep wounds inflicted by centuries of slavery. Her biographer suggests that Child's audacity may help explain her virtual erasure from mainstream U.S. history. Although both Child's book and those of the American Tract Society would sound condescending to modern ears, Child understood better than most of her contemporaries that Africans and African-Americans, whether slave or free, could be agents of their own lives, and not just grateful beneficiaries of kindly white people. Twelve passages in her textbook were penned by African-Americans. Her own respectful ten-page essay on Benjamin Banneker, a clockmaker and astronomer who was born to freed slaves in Maryland in 1732, attributes his success to his own talent and hard work. "He... never forgot one word of what he had learned at school. In this way, he came to have more knowledge than most of his white neighbors..." Child's retelling of Frederick Douglass' story describes how "Freddy," "had often...wondered why black children were born to be slaves; and now he heard his master say that if he learned to read it would spoil him for a slave." As soon as he could, Child suggests, Douglass made sure to "spoil" himself.

The cover of the Tract Society's speller depicted a dark-complected girl spelling out "Freedom" on a blackboard. Inside, the meaning of freedom is less clear. The preface notes, "while spelling and reading are the first things to be taught...it is believed that much practical information...cannot fail to be of great value to the freedmen in the new conditions into which Providence has raised them." Throughout, manual labor is valued above the acquisition of literacy, while piety, cleanliness, and deference trump knowledge. Some other Tract Society books written for freedmen portrayed Africa and Africans as inherently degraded.

Not all Northern whites were that patronizing. In a review published in the *American Freedman*, a monthly journal dedicated to Southern education, the American Tract Society's new texts were hailed for their usefulness and attractive presentation. "But why have a *Freedman's* Primer any more than a Dutchman's Primer or an Irishman's Primer?" asked the anonymous reviewer. "Are not the so-called Freedmen to learn the same language, spell the same words, and read the same literature as the rest of us?....Suppose the child was a slave, is that any reason why that odious recollection should be thrust in his face forever after?" Later, the Tract Society renamed its text "The Lincoln Spelling-Book." Meanwhile, freed people scrounged books wherever they could. Asked by the Freedmen's Bureau which books he used, a Georgia teacher said "any I can get."

The mission of the New York-based American Freedmen's and Union Commission, publisher of this review, was to educate more than four million former slaves, while also bring literacy to an estimated million white southerners who had traditionally also been deprived of effective education. Founded in February 1862, this organization took up the plight of "Contrabands" – slaves like William Henry Singleton who had escaped but might not yet be acknowledged by the Union. It was one of the largest among some three hundred private and governmental groups that sprang up to advance the education of freed slaves, white southern yeomen, or both. Leaders of A.F.U.C., as it called itself, included Reverend Lyman Abbott, a respected Congregationalist, and associate of Henry Ward Beecher, and long-time Boston abolition leader William Lloyd Garrison. Sojourner Truth, the outspoken former slave and feminist, was listed as an agent for the organization in the South. In 1867, U.S. Chief Justice Salmon P. Chase, who had served in Lincoln's cabinet, would become the organization's titular head.

This organization's avowed goal was to "aid and co-operate with the people of the South, without distinction of race or color, in the improvement of their condition upon the basis of industry, education, freedom, and Christian morality." They envisioned the spread of Horace Mann-style common schools open equally to the poorest blacks and whites, with lessons full of piety but free of sectarianism. Hundreds of teachers, both novices and veterans, were recruited and soon began fanning out across the South. Except in Maryland, where only "colored" teachers were requested, virtually all of the Union Commission's teaching recruits were white northerners.

Faced with behavior that ranged from derision to arson attacks, these women and men also endured smallpox outbreaks, searing heat, and shortages of textbooks, food, and clothing for themselves and their scholars. Depictions of female teachers as homely, foolish, or both were reworked along sectional lines. But there were satisfactions as well. In April, 1866, Carrie Blood, teaching sixty-eight African-American pupils in Poplar Grove, Virginia, happily reported that twenty-five of them were making excellent progress. As she explained, "The A B C class we have termed the 'McClellan'; the tablet reading in words of two or three letters, the 'Sheridan'; while 'Sherman' is applied to those who are beginning in the Primer; and the best readers glory in being subject to 'Grant.'" Miss Blood had not only cleverly introduced the names of Union generals but also ranked them by their relative importance in winning the war. Writing from New Bern, North Carolina after just four weeks on the job, "school ma'am" C.C. Thomas was concerned that freed men and women on a near-by 17,000-acre former plantation (almost certainly the same one that William Henry Singleton had earlier escaped) were not taking full advantage of proffered schooling. But she saw triumphs as well. "One look into a school-room full of men and women, almost right from the field, tired, sleepy, and hungry...puzzling their brains over the intricacies of 'A B C' would make the most slothful active....I anticipate great things for the next generation." Indeed, former slaves and their children poured into churches and make-shift school rooms by the thousands, eager to learn what was once forbidden. On a tour of Florida schools, E. C. Estes, secretary of the Union Commission, heard a Catholic priest from St. Augustine admit, "Our children won't study at all while the niggers are crazy to learn." However unfortunate the language, the priest's praise was both genuine and revealing.

Serious consideration of integrated learning for the South's most downtrodden was, to say the least, elusive. That August, *The American Freedman* published responses to a questionnaire titled "Our Future Work: The Best Means for its Prosecution." Much was at stake, particularly Southern literacy, or what Rev. Abbott, the general secretary, called education "of the ignorant without regard to color." Several directly tackled this delicate subject head-on. Was there "any probability of the poor whites, whether adults or children, consenting to come to school with colored persons?" His survey had been circulated to a friendly audience: mainly field agents for the Commission as well as some government personnel assigned to various sectors in the occupied South. Almost to a man and woman, the forty responders said that "There is no probability of the children of the poor whites attending the schools with colored persons." Most were certain that both races would protest such mingling. Only agent E. B. Adams insisted that integration was possible. That April, he had visited Miss Hosmer's school in tiny Summerville, South Carolina where sixty students, half of them white and half black, learned in apparent harmony. "They sat upon the same seats, studied the same books, recited the same classes...took the same recess...Two boys, who owned before the war seven slaves' patrimony, walked the greatest distance, six miles. Master and slave there sat side by side... one year after freedom." In historical hindsight, what amazes is not that mingling failed but that it was proposed and even attempted.

✎ ✎ ✎

Just twenty-two days after General Robert E. Lee surrendered at Appomattox, Mary Ames and Emily Bliss of Springfield,

Massachusetts boarded a steamer in New York City headed for Hilton Head, South Carolina. Both in their early thirties, and neither trained as school teachers, they had impulsively joined the ranks of "Yankee School Marms" sent to achieve educational miracles in the Reconstruction South. "Our families ridiculed our going and tried to stop us, prophesying our return in less than a month" Ames wrote in her diary, published three years after her death in 1903. The women soon learned that promises made to them by the U.S. Freedmen's Bureau in Boston had not been communicated to Bureau agents in South Carolina. Sent by night steamer to Charleston, the two young ladies found themselves sitting on a backless bench while all around them Union soldiers heading for discharge smoked, played cards, and swapped bawdy stories. It was, she wrote, "the longest night I ever knew." During a brief visit to some Charleston schools, they realized "how *un*fitted we were for teachers."

Soon Mary and the piteously homesick Emily joined 150 former slaves headed for Edisto, one of the coastal areas where General Sherman was resettling freedmen. The only whites allowed were military personnel, teachers, and supervisors, including Mr. Blake, "from New Haven, a pleasant young man" who was employed "to look after forlorn females who come as teachers." Edisto would be their home for eighteen months. Making do in an abandoned plantation house, the women dined on crackers and tea for three weeks, keeping a hammer near in case of trouble while they began cautiously interacting with a few of the ten thousand former slaves who lived and farmed on the island. In a badly-damaged church, they soon began teaching nine boys and six girls. Wrote Ames, "One or two knew their letters. None could read." Likewise, some were "decently clad"; others were "filthy and nearly naked." She resolved to teach "cleanliness as well as spelling." A day later, thirteen more students appeared. Two had walked five miles; two others could already read.. A black Baptist minister who ran his own school on the island agreed to collaborate with Ames and Bliss, once they had explained their Unitarian creed to his satisfaction.

By mid-May, heat, rattlesnakes, and all manner of insects were posing new challenges for the Massachusetts women, making the half-mile walk to their school "tiresome." They arrived one day to find a student body of sixty-six, including some boys too unruly for Emily to control. Not all the news was bad. The novice teachers were elated when Mr. Blake showed up in June, saying he was "surprised and delighted with our school; he said Miss K.'s and Miss S's school bore no comparison, — and *they* certified schoolma'ams!" By then, sixty or seventy children were showing up regularly and adult evening classes were also well attended "All are respectful and eager to learn. We notice that all the children and grown-ups also hold their books sidewise; when we asked why, a man answered 'we wish to learn to read on all sides.'"

Very soon this teaching experiment was already in serious jeopardy as the Freedmen's Bureau curtailed food provisions. Five remaining Edisto teachers subsisted on watermelons and weevil-infested bread dipped in molasses until a private Boston freedmen's aid group contributed a hundred dollars. The plight of Edisto's freedpeople was dire. Ames' diary chronicles much death and disease, most due to poverty. Some of the women's most promising scholars were among the sick and dying. In mid-October, General O. O. Howard, head of the Freedmen's Bureau, arrived to break the news that President Johnson had pardoned Edisto's former squires who would soon return. Freedpeople unwilling to work for wages on the plantations would have to go elsewhere. In her diary, Ames noted many spelling lapses committed in the Edisto freedmen's appeal to the President ("peple," "Carlina," and "privalage" for example) but her nit-picking was tempered by real sorrow for the many African-Americans whom she had indeed come to respect.

Still the women soldiered on, attracting 120 students in a crumbling manor, but soon learned that most were there in hopes of acquiring clothing and supplies, not education. Ames was briefly buoyed in December when a group of black soldiers happily accepted books in return for fixing the women's smoky chimney. But the task of teaching "the alphabet to the little children" proved to be a casualty of the recent "smallpox vacation…"

As Edisto's whites reclaimed the island, the Yankee teachers, clearly unwelcome, "said good-by to Edisto and our negro friends" in the last week of September, 1866. Mary Ames never married. "Strong, brave, and helpful," she became a beloved school teacher in her native Springfield and dedicated the proceeds of her diary to Virginia's Hampton College, founded in 1868 as one of America's first schools of higher learning for African-Americans.

After the war, white Southern women supplanted despised "Yankee" teachers and by 1880 were a majority of the region's school teachers. As Reconstruction-era educators had predicted, school segregation quickly, although not universally, became the norm. This promised new opportunities for African-American educators, but also meant Ku Klux Klan attacks (mostly directed at black male teachers) and meager budgets and facilities.

Even aside from the tense and unequal racial situation, public education in the Southern states would continue to be plagued with sparse populations and pockets of rural poverty that made it very difficult to assure universal instruction even for one race, if not both. Education took root in many of the larger cities, especially in more education-minded states, including North Carolina, Georgia, and Virginia. But as hated Reconstruction era educational initiatives faded, both white and black schools in most of the former Confederacy were fiscally starved by state governors and legislatures who considered public school funding a luxury at best and "socialistic" at worst. School terms had peaked at a hundred days a year during Reconstruction but would not equal that modest educational achievement until the early twentieth century.

There was some progress: the 1880 U. S. Census had counted seventy percent of black adults in the South as illiterate but by 1891, black illiteracy had fallen to fifty-eight percent, and white illiteracy to thirty-one percent. Yet just four percent of Southern white teenagers and less than a half-percent of black teens were enrolled in high school. The 1900 U.S. Census revealed that less than forty percent of white children aged five to nine-years-old, and barely a quarter of black children of the same age were attending school during their prime reading and spelling years. Not until the early the twentieth century did Southern educational reformers begin to find ways to improve public and rural education. In Greensboro, the 1902 graduating class of North Carolina Normal and Industrial School for Women was galvanized into action when their president exhorted them to "revolutionize" the state's public education system. Soon thousands of white women in several Southern states were working to improve school facilities. In 1903, Southern educational reformer Edgar G. Murphy told the National Education Association (NEA) in Boston that education expenditures in his region were just $4.50 per pupil, at a time when average per-pupil expenditures in other regions ranged from $21.14 to $31. But he was hopeful. Alabama had recently doubled its appropriations, he said, and other southern states had already begun or were poised to follow the state's example. Said Murphy, "I find no hopelessness in the illiteracy of the South... because it is the illiteracy not of the degenerate, but simply of the unstarted."

Many voices called for industrial education for all Southerners, especially poor whites and blacks who might otherwise "be kept as a tenant or farmhand, to his own injury and the incalculable harm [to] the South itself." Booker T. Washington, born a slave in Virginia in 1856, attributed his success as a leader and educator to literacy taboos that had made him, along with many other African-Americans, all the more eager to learn. As a child, he was allowed to joke, fish, even wrestle with white children, but forbidden to enter the schoolhouse or open a book. Like Frederick Douglass before him, Washington "resolved that I should never be satisfied until I learned what this dangerous practice was like." During the Civil War and after, he wrote, "the hidden book that had been tucked away under the floor or in an old trunk or had been concealed in a stump or between mattresses, suddenly came out of its hiding place and was put to work...." He praised men and women who "would fasten their primers between the ploughshares, so they could read as they ploughed. I have seen Negro coal miners trying to spell out the words of a little reading book by the dim light of a miner's lamp."

Washington himself had been one of those miners before he attained his own education in West Virginia, followed by the respect and clout he earned in Alabama and across the nation as president of the Tuskegee Institute. A prolific and polished writer and orator, he favored British spellings – words such as "coloured," "labour," "centre," and "plough." But his graduates were taught to aspire to modest and practical goals, not bold forays into the learned spheres and leadership roles that white men still jealously guarded. In a telling 1897 exchange with Henry Villard, one of his many white benefactors, Washington apologized on behalf of a young woman student who had apparently overstepped the bounds of what was considered appropriate for a female African-American in the era of Jim Crow.

Born in Bavaria, Villard was a journalist and Civil War correspondent who later made a fortune in railroads and bought the *New York Evening Post*. Reporting in 1863 from the liberated Sea Islands, home then to some nine thousand black people, the twenty-eight year-old Villard was clearly appalled and shaken by what he perceived as their savage ignorance. When a white chaplain asked "Brother" Villard to address "our colored brethren," he "used the simplest possible language," but "felt sure that I was not understood." He added, "It seemed to me that the efforts of the volunteer male and female teachers from the North to instill even a little rudimentary knowledge into the skulls of the adults were bound to prove futile, and so they did." For a man of his era, however, Villard was hardly a racist. His wife, Helene, was abolitionist William Lloyd Garrison's daughter. His son Oswald became a founding member of the NAACP and collaborated with black Harvard-trained sociologist W.E.B. Du Bois who was Booker T. Washington's most trenchant critic.

The tiff between the railroad baron and the nation's leading black educator emerged in June, 1897 when Henry Villard sent

Washington (whom he addressed as "Dear Sir") a promised check for $100, but added that it came with conditions. Villard praised the Tuskegee promise, which he defined as "an elementary education coupled with a training in domestic arts, agriculture, and mechanical trades, so as to...set a good example...to their race." But he was upset by a letter he had received some months earlier from a Tuskegee student, "a young woman, who evidently not only has an insufficient knowledge of English grammar and is even unable to spell correctly, and yet writes me that her last studies have been in 'Natural Philosophy, Ancient History, Algebra and Grammar'" Other educators, said Villard, agreed that such overreaching would be a "travesty of higher education..." and warned that his financial support might cease if it was allowed to continue.

Washington's response a week later trod a fine line between meekness and affirmation. "You will find at Tuskegee as [at] most schools I think, those who have imperfectly mastered what they have gone over, especially will you find those who are weak in spelling and the use of the English language, and it is for this reason that I have never permitted any language to be taught at Tuskegee except English," he wrote. He described the offending student as "ambitious" and prone to exaggeration, and assured Villard that "your criticism has done us good and I thank you for it." Keeping white magnates happy was ever a risky proposition.

In 1908, the National Education Association held its annual meeting in Cleveland, Ohio. Founded in 1857, mainly by northerners who accepted some black educators to their ranks and decried rules forbidding slave education, the NEA was large, liberal, and influential enough to have Booker T. Washington deliver the keynote address. According to the white-owned *Cleveland Plain Dealer* and the African-American *Cleveland Journal*, some six thousand delegates applauded the nation's most famous black figure: the educator who had controversially dined at the White House with President Theodore Roosevelt just five years earlier. Washington made the case for more energetic efforts to improve Negro education, saying. "These millions of my race can be made useless or useful....They can be made potent factors in the intelligence of our country, or they can become a load of ignorance dragging down our civilization. Which shall it be?"

An answer was near at hand, and it nearly eclipsed Washington's speech. A day earlier, Marie C. Bolden, a fourteen-year-old Cleveland eighth grader, had won a spelling contest as part of the NEA's 1908 gathering. She apparently correctly spelled, on paper and orally, all 414 words that NEA experts had recently decided were most important to know. Her feat assured victory for the sixteen-member Cleveland team as they outspelled teams from Pittsburgh and Erie, Pennsylvania, and New Orleans.

Dr. Washington departed from his text to acknowledge the young woman's triumph. "I think you will admit that we spell out of the same spelling book that you do," he told his predominantly white audience. "And I think you will also admit that we spell a little better." The NEA delegates and Clevelanders erupted in cheers. As the *New York Times* headlined, Marie Bolden was a "colored girl." Her father was a letter carrier and her mother once ran a home for aged colored people. "I did not enter the spelling contest for personal glory," said Marie, "but to try to help bring honor to my teacher and my school." She attributed her stunning success to her regular reading of newspapers.

Bolden's triumph almost reignited civil war between Cleveland and New Orleans, whose all-white team finished in third-place after misspelling sixty-six words. One of Cleveland's black newspapers gleefully reprinted a New Orleans newspaper's complaints, focused on both Yankees and Negroes. Said the Southern paper: "It is not likely that the school children of New Orleans will ever again compete in a northern spelling bee, certainly not one held in a Negrophile city like Cleveland, where public schools are mixed...

and social equality is taught." Admitting to an on-going financial crisis in the New Orleans schools, the paper instead focused on race. "We doubt if there are a dozen white people in New Orleans who would for a moment encourage the idea of a mixed black and white spelling bee," they wrote. The "great aim of the Negroes and carpetbaggers," the article continued, was to "force mixed schools upon us." Cleveland, they added, was historically almost as "extreme on the Negro question as the most radical portions of New England." Finally, said the paper, "Our school children should no more enter spelling bees with Negroes in Cleveland than they would think of doing so in New Orleans." A further insult to the Crescent City occurred in August 1908 when New Orleans school and city officials scrambled to forbid a "great spelling bee in honor of Marie C. Bolden," organized by New Orleans' African-American students.

A nasty coda, playing out in the Cleveland black community briefly threatened to ruin the young speller's triumph. Though the five-year-old *Journal,* a staunch ally of Booker T. Washington, hailed Marie Bolden wholeheartedly, the influential black *Cleveland Gazette,* owned and published since 1883 by Harry C. Smith, treated the girl's triumph as "much ado about nothing," or even a sham, possibly because Smith, a charter member of the NAACP, was no admirer of Dr. Washington.

But Bolden's widely-noted achievement ultimately could not be denied. The NEA bestowed a gold medal, and both blacks and whites gave her a parade. The Cleveland Association of Colored Men took up a collection for an additional medal. Finally, Cleveland public schools' assistant superintendent W.E. Hicks took Bolden's side. "Hundreds of clippings from newspapers everywhere have given you the credit of championship," he wrote on July 26. Apparently alluding to the Pittsburgh spelling team's assertion that the official pronouncer had confused the spellings of "capital" and "Capitol," Hicks affirmed Bolden saying, "Even Pittsburg [sic]...gave their medals to the girl who spelled 'capitol, as 'capitol."

The NEA spelling bee that created such a furor seems to have been the first and last one attempted by the teacher organization. Not until seventeen years later would the *Louisville Courier-Journal*, the leading newspaper in the considerably segregated state of Kentucky, revive the idea of a national spelling contest. Simply put, Marie C. Bolden, champion speller of 1908 and a credit to her race and education must be hailed the very first winner of an American national Spelling Bee.

4 | The Peculiar Life and Near-Death of Spelling Reform

On August 22, 1906, President Theodore Roosevelt sent a brief note to Brander Matthews, a Columbia University English professor who was TR's longtime friend and his authority on matters linguistic. "It may interest you to know," wrote the President, who was summering at his estate in Oyster Bay, New York, "that the Public Printer has been instructed to follow the rules of your new Spelling Reform Association, and [my secretary] himself an advanced spelling reformer, will hereafter see that the President in his correspondence spells the way you say he ought to."

When news broke days later that the president, a progressive Republican and accomplished author, but indifferent speller, had ordered executive agencies to use three hundred "reformed" spellings, the popular and pugnacious TR quickly became a laughingstock. "King Ted" was ridiculed by newspapers nationwide and on both sides of the Atlantic. Soon, Professor Matthews was disingenuously telling the *New York Times* that Roosevelt's adoption of reformed spellings was an "entire surprise." In fact, Matthews, an ardent advocate of spelling reform since at least 1892, had visited TR at the White House in the spring of 1906. "Of course, I am with you on the spelling," the President told his old friend. Later he sent Matthews a draft of his executive order.

Making fun of Roosevelt, whose coterie of "out-law" academic experts comprised the Spelling Board, proved almost too easy. Roosevelt's surname name alone set off gleeful rounds of "simplification," even among those who were usually friends and allies. One of the few on either side of the Atlantic who defended Roosevelt was Anglo-Irish writer George Bernard Shaw. Despite what he considered major defects in the details of Roosevelt's reforms, Shaw penned a long letter to the *Times* of London in which he assailed the "outburst of ignorance and folly" that had greeted "President Ruzvelt (if he will allow me to simplify him to that extent)...." Engrained notions of social class, Shaw observed, are a major obstacle to simplified spelling. Said Shaw, "most Englishmen and women would almost rather die than be convicted of speaking like costermongers and flower girls...," anticipating by some eight years his own Cockney lass who learns to speak "proper" in his play *Pygmalion*.

As the torrent of parody and criticism continued well into 1907, a strange populism seemed to take hold as newspapers that usually positioned themselves as the colloquial and often sensational voice of ordinary people turned into saviors of received spelling. As a professor of journalism noted years later, newspapers actually stood to benefit from simpler, shorter, and snappier spellings. Yet, some of America's most respected language experts found themselves depicted as foolish, overweening, or even corrupt for wanting to make spelling easier for ordinary Americans. Most major U.S. newspapers sounded much like their supercilious British cousins, blaming overreaching linguists and other authorities for enlisting the President in a misguided scheme to "dumb-down" English by removing silent letters and otherwise perverting the sacred tongue. David Starr

SPELLING REFORM BECOMES STRENUOUS.

Andrew and Teddy Redo the three 'Rs'

Jordan, president of Stanford University, was hailed by newspapers coast to coast when he withdrew from the Simplified Spelling Board in November, 1906, saying that he had not endorsed the by-then infamous list. Even the *Chicago Tribune*, whose publishers had flirted with spelling simplification in the 1870s and '80s, and would do so again in the Thirties, joined in the general censure and amusement.

In Washington, epicenter of this spelling "quake," cartoons and doggerel spilled from the pages of periodicals. At the 23rd annual Gridiron Dinner at Washington's New Willard Hotel, more than a hundred politicians and journalists laughed with and at the

President. Never was this "stag" event's theme more obvious. The program and menu both featured "simplified spelling," of which this is but the first course:

> The Simple Speller
> and
> Gridiron Dikshunary
> Being a Kompilation of Wordz now
> Properly Spelt for the First Time in
> History with their Korrekt
> Definishunz...
> In the VI year uv the rane uv Theodore
> Rozavelt

Careful readers will surely notice that the parodists "misspelled" Kompilation, which should certainly be "Kompilashun." And how about "simple," "their," and "year"? Surely these needed to be "simpl," "thar," and "yeer."

Days later, the U.S. House of Representatives' Appropriations Committee, returned from an extended recess to hold hearings on the new spelling list, even though Roosevelt's executive order was not technically subject to Congressional review. More than new spellings were at stake; so too was a substantial raise pending for Charles A. Stillings, the federal government's Public Printer. As the person designated to implement Roosevelt's order, Stillings was grilled at length on the potential expense of new printing plates and fielded concerns that each branch of government might adopt a different spelling scheme. Many legislators seemed to believe that the president's initiative was an effort to subvert the American language, discombobulate public education, and force millions to replace all their books and dictionaries at great expense.

Just before Christmas, the House resolved that all government printing "should observe and adhere to the standard of orthography prescribed in generally accepted dictionaries..." Only one member,

Frederick H. Gillet, a Republican from western Massachusetts, rose to defend the President on final passage, even though he thought that the word "through," respelled on the Roosevelt list as "thru," should actually be spelled "throo." (For his trouble, the *Washington Post* would misspell Rep. Gillet's name as "Gillette" in all its coverage).

Stillings' $1,500 raise was approved; the President, claiming to be "much amused by the uproar in the House," backed down, although he reserved himself the right to use reformed spelling in correspondence that did not go through the Public Printer. A week later, Senator Henry Cabot Lodge Sr., usually a reliable ally of the President, asked the Public Printer to redo a "simplified" Panama Canal message that Roosevelt had sent to the Senate during those brief but halcyon weeks of the new spelling.

It must have galled a President who had in 1906 marched from triumph to triumph as he married off daughter Alice at the White House, signed the nation's first Pure Food and Drug Act, traveled to Panama to view construction on his audacious Canal project, and won a Nobel Peace Prize for ending the Russo-Japanese War. But Roosevelt's usually "Bully Pulpit" collapsed when he attempted limited changes to the American language.

Also enmeshed in this onslaught of press and public ridicule was America's wealthiest industrialist, the Scottish-born steel magnate Andrew Carnegie who in early 1906, at the behest of Matthews and Melvil Dewey, had agreed to underwrite new spelling initiatives to the tune of $25,000 a year. (Dewey, the autocratic father of the Dewey decimal system that isstill used in some libraries, often rendered his name as "Dui," and required his family to communicate with him in his preferred mode of simple spelling). Carnegie was no academic. A weaver's son, he left school at thirteen when his family immigrated to America, having "wrestled" with English and knowing "as little of what it was designed to teach as children usually do." He often used spellings of his own devising, including "bild," "spelt," and "erth." The press quickly added to this list "Androo

Karnege" and savaged his presumed efforts to "buy" changes in orthodox orthography.

A full year after the President gave up his reform proposal, Carnegie was still a figure of fun. In December, 1907, writer and humorist Mark Twain, himself both an excellent speller and a charter member of the Simplified Spelling Board, tweaked Carnegie at the dedication of a New York City engineers' club, built with the retired steel man's recent million dollar gift. A crowd of some three hundred enjoyed Twain's ruminations. "You might think that [Carnegie] had never committed a crime in his life," joked Twain, adding "But no – look at his pestiferous simple spelling... He's got us all so we can't spell anything." The real problem, Twain wisecracked, was that Carnegie and his fellow reformers "attacked orthography at the wrong end...Let's get Mr. Carnegie to reform the alphabet, and we'll pray for him if he'll take the risk."

Making English easier to read and spell meshed with Carnegie's on-going efforts to enhance worldwide understanding. His annual contributions for Simplified Spelling overlapped with his creation in 1910 of the Carnegie Endowment for International Peace. But by 1915, Carnegie, utterly disappointed with the lack of results, ended his financial support for simpler spelling, saying he had been "patient long enuf."

Roosevelt's ordeal was also not quite over. As the controversy had boiled over in October, 1906, Owen Wister, best-selling author of *The Virginian* and "one of the foremost of Our Younger Writers," attacked spelling simplification in the *New York Times'* Saturday Review of Books. The English language's greatest strength, said Wister, "lie[s] in the 'inconsistency' it has drawn from its many ancestors; a language that can use Greek, Latin, Danish, Saxon, and French...in the vast richness of its eloquence, and that surpasses any the world has known..."

Months later, Wister rekindled the general amusement when he published a brief farce entitled *How Doth the Simple Spelling Bee*. Appearing first in the *Saturday Evening Post*, it quickly became an illustrated hardcover priced at fifty cents and widely reviewed in Britain as well as the U. S. Although famous as a "Western" author, Wister was an upper-middle class Philadelphian with family roots in the Confederacy who by 1904, according to a biographer, opposed immigration and embraced other socially conservative views. But Wister was also one of Theodore Roosevelt's dearest friends from Harvard where they had met in 1879. "Dan" as Wister was known to Roosevelt, was regularly invited to the White House and Oyster Bay. Wister dedicated *The Virginian* to TR and wrote a fond memoir of their enduring friendship eleven years after Roosevelt's death in 1919.

Wister was no Mark Twain and his attempts at humor in this little book veered into whimsy. The press and public agreed that *How Doth*, although a mere confection, was "a clever comment upon a passing phase" likely to kill spelling reform if it was not already dead. "Every Carnegie Library should have a copy," the *Newark News* wrote snidely. The book's shady mastermind is one Masticator B. Fellows, "President and Proprietor of Chickle University, Arkansopolis." Portrayed as a chewing gum millionaire, mass-market educator, and Washington power broker, Fellows aims for world domination via publicity. Spelling reform is but one of his schemes. In the book's cover illustrations by F. R. Gruger, Fellows looks more like John D. Rockefeller than Andrew Carnegie, but sounds more demagogical than either. Deluded academic theorists of spelling reform with such names as Kibosh, Maverick, Egghorn, Totts, and Dudelsacker, bear the brunt of Wister's genial sarcasm. Addressing the professors he has cajoled, bribed, or threatened, Fellows declares, "Everything is getting better. Man is getting better. Woman is getting better. Life, Liberty, Happiness – all getting better....Then why not English Spelling?"

Roosevelt likely ignored his old friend's ridicule, even as a Philadelphia newspaper wondered if TR was reading this "little satire of spelling reform." But by April, 1907 Roosevelt had clearly suffered entirely enough. "Dear Brander," he wrote to Prof. Matthews, his other persistent literary friend, "I do not think it best that just at

present I should say anything more about the Simplified Spelling."
For years afterward, "Roosevelt's List" would be invoked as a warning against spelling reform enthusiasm. In the wake of Roosevelt's, Matthews', and Carnegie's debacle, orthographical reform efforts older than the American nation itself faltered, even as proposals for more rational, simpler, or more efficient spelling would continue to tantalize.

Nearly forgotten amid the grandstanding were the actual three hundred words selected by the Spelling Board and so briefly adopted by the President. Just three thousand Executive department workers would use the simpler spellings. Roosevelt would insist in his August 27 letter of instruction to the Public Printer that the list represented "very moderate and common-sense" changes with "not the slightest intention to do anything revolutionary..." It was true that the new rules underlying the infamous list were quite modest by the standards of many earlier plans. Stillings told Congressional critics that more than half of the three hundred "reformed" words were already regularly used in government publications. Yet there remained much to chew and choke on.

There were, for starters, some controversial rules. "Use -t in place of -ed for the past or past participle of verbs ending in s, sh, or p... *dipt, dript, prest, husht, washt....*" And, "When you can replace a -gh with an -f, do it. Better still, get rid of -gh altogether." Or this: "From words spelled with "sc"... omit the -c," leading, in one example, to "sithe" (scythe). The list fairly buzzed as "z" replaced a great many esses. Meanwhile, virtually all uses of the hard -c became -k's. Many letters were omitted on account of silence, such as the terminal -e and -ue endings of words such as catalogue and demagogue. Some rules showed little concern for the ways in which consonants and vowels, even if silent, interact to produce the sound and sense of English.

Even many of the chosen three-hundred were problematic. While everyday words such as "thru" and "tho" got the worst press (although "thru," at least, was already common and has proved quite durable in colloquial usage) one must wonder how often federal clerks had to deal with such words as "Eolian" (formerly Aeolian), "lacrimal" (formerly lachrymal), or "woful" in place of woeful, or even the British-inflected woefull.

TR was a popular president, but it seems unlikely that any political figure could ordain language rules that generations of American writers, rhetoricians and grammarians could not undo. Even slangy newspapermen and authors who celebrated the quaint vocal and spelling styling of Hoosiers, former slaves, grizzled prospectors, and one-time Mississisippiipi river rats like Mark Twain, took cover in orthographic orthodoxy. Mr. Twain was revealed to really be Samuel Langhorne Clemens after all.

Neither Matthews, Carnegie, nor Roosevelt, of course, were America's first or most zealous spelling transformers: Noah Webster had long since laid claim to that distinction. Ideas for improving the language were rife in early nineteenth century America. New spelling schemes proliferated with as much vigor and variety as did proposals for utopian communities. Cincinnati, one of the nation's fastest-growing cities, was a hub of new spelling ideas, many of them inspired by and closely linked to the huge success of Isaac Pitman, an Englishman who had in 1837 devised a new system for quickly recording speech on paper. It was initially called "Stenographic Sound-Hand." Among his earliest American devotees was Bostonian abolitionist lawyer Stephen Pearl Andrews, who encountered the "Pitmanian project" while attending the 1843 World Anti-Slavery Convention in London. The next year, Andrews, inventor of a simplified language he called "Alwato," prepared the first American Pitman instruction book. "Pitmania" was truly afoot.

Pitman was a lifelong crusader for spelling reform and staunch proponent of public education. He attracted a galaxy of adherents and true believers on both sides of the Atlantic. Many saw in his new shorthand system a fix for the failings of standard spelling. Pitman, like Andrew Carnegie after him, was the son of a handloom weaver whose formal education ended at age thirteen. A voracious reader, Pitman was aggravated by "misleading or ambiguous spellings." A teetotaler who also abjured tobacco, Pitman was an early vegetarian and controversially adopted the Swedenborgian faith in his twenties. He would be knighted for his stenographic achievements in 1894, three years before his death.

Rather than somehow trying to align with standard spelling, Pitman's system was based entirely on word sounds: phonetics. Looking much like squiggles or Chinese characters stripped of their ornate calligraphy, the forty characters of Pitman shorthand became especially popular in the United States when Benn Pitman, Isaac's younger brother who was also an accomplished stenographer, permanently relocated to Cincinnati in 1852. The younger Pitman began publishing his *Phonographic Magazine* there. He also founded a Phonetic Institute, and was a stenographer at the post-war trial of President Lincoln's assassins. Benn Pitman lived long enough to correspond with Andrew Carnegie on the advantages and drawbacks of the English alphabet and to applaud President Roosevelt's simpli-fied spelling edict, saying, "I am delighted. I knew it would come. It may take a century – [one] cannot change a system — or a lack of system — in a day." Cincinnati was also home to Elias Longley, a printer, stenographer, and committed spelling reformer. His wife, Elizabeth Margaret Vater, shared Longley's enthusiasm. She was an early adopter of the mechanical typewriter and inventor of the "All-Finger" method, an early stab at touch typing. Longley's *Wecli Fonetic Advocat*, which he published with one of his five printer brothers in "SinSinati," was described on its masthead as "A jurnal ov N[u]z, S[i]ens, Lituratur, Educa [shun] and Reform." (Brackets are used here in place of the special symbols that Longley devised for his thirty-nine letter alphabet). His four-page "Volyum V, Numbur 15," published on "Saturda, Novembur 6, 1852," reprinted an article from Benn Pitman's *Phonetic Journal* and reported this breaking news: "Horas Man haz acsepted [the] a[p]tment ov President ov Antioc Colej, at Yelo Springz O."

In 1895, Longley, by then in his seventies and living in Los Angeles, sent a long letter to the *New York Times*. His spelling was standard but his message was fierce. He demanded to know why current advocates of orthographical reform, most of them academics who by then were getting mostly reverent attention from the Eastern press, had forgotten their crusading forebears.

Longley was referring to news of "an important conference of authors and literary men," among them Roosevelt's pal, Brander Matthews, who had assembled at Columbia College on May 31 to take action on spelling reform. The "irregularities" of English orthography, these organizers declared, were "an abstacle [sic] to the spread of Anglo-Saxon thought."

As a pioneering printer who had spent fifty years toiling for spelling reform, Longley expressed more than a whiff of class resentment. He wanted to know why he had not been invited to the Columbia gathering, but promised to forgive this neglect if the new breed of orthographers "will accept what has already been accomplished." His letter included a copy of his 1849 American Phonetic Alphabet of thirty-nine letters, grouped into vowels, diphthongs, semi-vowels, aspirates, explodents, and continuants. He ended by warning that spelling reform would never succeed if its advocates overlooked pioneering elders and failed to cooperate with peers. Longley died at age 75 in January, 1899, his challenge almost certainly ignored. At least a tiny obituary notice identified him as "a prominent advocate of spelling reform."

If reformed English spelling could be a "band of union," as Noah Webster had hoped, it could also celebrate singularity. In 1845, Brigham Young, who had succeeded the murdered founder Joseph Smith as Prophet of the Church of Jesus Christ of Latter-day Saints – the Mormons – became fascinated by the potential of reformed spelling. He was introduced to the idea by George Darling Watt, a skilled Pitman phonographer who had grown up poor in Manchester, England and was among the first group of British converts to the Mormon faith. Young was excited by the idea of a spelling system that might attract both the unlettered and non-English speakers to Mormonism, and would imbue Mormons, especially children, with special knowledge that would be inscrutable to gentiles.

More pressing issues intervened in 1846 as Young led his embattled flock from Nauvoo, Illinois, to Great Salt Lake, then Mexican territory, creating the new community of Deseret. Once settled, Young returned to spelling with renewed enthusiasm that apparently was never widely shared by the larger Mormon community. In 1852, he urged the regents of the University of Deseret to create a new alphabet, and assigned Watt to implement the project. Fellow committee members argued successfully against simply adopting Pitman's signs, calling them "too similar to the present English language."

The result was a Deseret alphabet of thirty-eight letters, two fewer than Pitman's system, and bearing only a passing resemblance either to Pitman's markings or standard English letters. It included symbols for six long and six short vowel sounds, five double sounds, and twenty-one consonant and "portmanteau" sounds including -eng as in length and ch- as in cheese. Special typefaces had to be manufactured in St. Louis at great expense. The church-owned *Deseret News* in 1859 published a number of articles in this new writing, but not until 1868, when Young insisted, were First and Second children's readers and large portions of the *Book of Mormon* published in the new alphabet.

Watt had by then quit his clerkship in an apparent disagreement with Young over compensation. In May, 1874, he was excommunicated after dallying with a heretic Mormon splinter group. Any remaining interest in the Deseret alphabet collapsed after Brigham Young's death in 1877. Although Young was clearly trying to solidify a unique identity for Mormons through language, his expressed goals of easing education and making the language more effective and efficient shared much with Noah Webster's grand scheme of one nation, undivided by the English language's peculiarities and inconsistencies.

𝄞 𝄞 𝄞

As the short-lived Mormon alphabet faded out west, in major universities primarily in the East and Midwest, new advocates of spelling restructuring were mustering the most successful effort yet to challenge and change American orthography. Hinterland printers, like Elias Longley and Watt, and oddballs, like South Carolinian Thomas Grimke, an educational reformer, who, along with his much better known abolitionist sister, Angelina, shared an aversion to silent letters, had dominated this discussion in the years before the Civil War. A high point for pre-war spelling reform came together in an 1852 Phonetic National Convention in New York City headed by Stephen Pearl Andrews, Isaac Pitman's adherent. In "very able and pointed address," Andrews reminded the assembly that English was poised to become a universal language, making phonetics training all the more urgent. As part of the proceedings, a group of youngsters dubbed the "celebrated Boston Phonetic Children" performed a sort of spelling bee in reverse as they used their knowledge of Pitman characters to quickly decode such words as "daguerreotype," garnering "bursts of applause." At this same gathering, a Providence, Rhode Island teacher told the assembly in Clinton Hall that his use of phonetic practices had entirely eliminated lisping and stammering among his students.

𝄞 𝄞 𝄞

The post-war years would soon usher in a rather different set of language and spelling concerns, spearheaded by academic and professional specialists. Phonetics and phonetic spelling schemes had long been considered the bailiwick of "half-educated" outsiders.

But by the 1870s, some were bemoaning traditional orthography as "much more an aristocratic luxury than a popular benefit" for the muscular modern nation aborning. New learned societies were acknowledging that the languages of technical expertise, journalism, and even some kinds of slang could prove beneficial for the largest English-speaking nation, awash in eager emigrants, and poised for world power.

The American Philological Association was founded on July 29, 1869 at a church in Poughkeepsie, New York by forty-four scholars, many of whom were immersed in classical Greek and Latin. But that very day, members discussed the "possibility and desirability" of phonetic spelling of English. The association's interest in English orthography would endure into the next century, thanks in large measure to Francis A. March, a scholar of Anglo-Saxon. He would spend much of his fifty-five year career at Lafayette College energetically advancing spelling reform. Professor March and the college proved to be a perfect fit. March, an expert in an ancient tongue, developed this nationalistic theme and nurtured it until his death at age eighty-six in 1911.

Like so many who distinguished themselves in various arenas of nineteenth century reform, March was a New Englander, born in Worcester, Massachusetts in a family that traced its roots to the Puritan migration. His father, a cutlery manufacturer brought low by a thieving partner and a disastrous fire, was unable to send his brilliant fifteen-year-old son to college until a local benefactor paid his way into Amherst College, the school that Noah Webster had helped found in 1821. March attended lectures by the elderly Webster and remained loyal to many of Webster's ideas and ideals.

Graduating in 1845 as class valedictorian, March tutored at Amherst and several private academies and studied law before joining the Lafayette faculty. In 1857, he was named Professor of the English Language, the first such designation in the United States, thus fulfilling the hopes of the college's founders and astonishing an educational establishment still devoted to the primacy of Greek and

Latin. It was from that platform that Francis Andrew March would launch his crusade for spelling reform, based on his intensive study of Anglo-Saxon and English speech and literature.

Both spelling reform and Professor March gained a national and international stage in August, 1876, when Philadelphia's Centennial Exposition celebrating America's hundredth birthday drew a four-day International Convention for the Amendment of English Orthography. More than a hundred delegates from across the U. S. and a smattering of Europeans gathered at the Atlas Hotel on Elm Street, just outside the Centennial Grounds. About a quarter of the delegates were women, most of them primary and secondary school teachers.

Playing a key role was New-Yorker Eliza Boardman Burns who was chosen as vice president of the new Spelling Reform Association. Recognized by Benn Pitman as a leader in promoting American adoption of the Pitman system, Mrs. Burns, who often spelled her name "Burnz," helped to develop the reformed spelling used in the Centennial proceedings. Two years later, she had the unique honor (for a woman) to be attacked by name in the newspaper by a foe of phonetic spelling who identified himself only as "R.G.W." Decrying the current "phonetic mania," he dismissed Mrs. Burns' proposed forty-seven character "Anglo-American" alphabet as excessively complicated. English, he predicted, would gradually reform itself.

At least one African-American, educator J. B. Towe of Norfolk, Virginia, took part in the convention. According to the official proceedings (rendered entirely in a semi-phonetic "reformed" spelling that organizers cheerfully admitted was riddled with inconsistencies) "Mr. Towe (colord) spoke for his rase, and ov the great work to be dun in educating the colord peeple of the South. They spel naturally in the simplest manner, and cannot be persuaded that silent letterz hav eny use." This statement was not as condescending as it sounds; it would have been apparent to this assemblage that African-American freedmen and women were already well ahead of their white brethren in reconstructing the English language on a more rational basis.

Among the eminences in attendance was Melvil Dewey, the Amherst College librarian who would later play a central role in Carnegie's and Roosevelt's list. But March carried the day.

His was no theoretical discussion of phonemes and etymologies but a full-voiced call to action in a nation where the 1870 Census had identified 5.5 million illiterates in a population of forty million. Literacy, March told the assembled school teachers and academics, is a "mighty machinery working for the future," a machine even more powerful and important than the telegraph and steam engine that were the pride of nineteenth century technology. He added, sounding very much like Webster:

> We ought to improve our spelling from patriotic and philanthropic motives.
> If these do not move us, it may be worthwhile to remember that...we throw away $15,000,000 a year paying teachers for addling the brains of our children with bad spelling, and at least $100,000,000 more paying printers and publishers for sprinkling our books and papers with silent letters.

When March inveighed against "the evils of bad" spelling," he was not scolding a lazy child who botched his spelling test, but rather challenging governments, publishers, and teachers to jettison the "irrational" orthography of English and in so doing make spelling mistakes impossible. And his pragmatic prescriptions for reform invoked values dear to American hearts: fiscal prudence, efficiency, and a path to cultural supremacy. At the conclusion of the convention, March was elected first president of the Spelling Reform Association.

March had called teachers of the young "our best hope" and indeed quite a few teachers and teaching organizations across the nation responded enthusiastically at the convention and afterward. March took up his spelling reform mandate with vigor, producing streams of pamphlets and articles for such opinion makers as John

Eaton who was Commissioner of Education, then housed in the U. S. Department of the Interior. Meanwhile, he was gratified to report in 1878 that teachers and state and local education departments from Michigan to Virginia, from Maryland to Missouri, and on to Iowa, were raising their voices in favor of spelling reform. A group of Massachusetts teachers even spent the day after the Christmas of 1878 discussing the topic. Standard spelling, most seemed to agree, was the cause of "alarming" illiteracy among American youth, and consumed a full two years of schooling.

March was also one of six Pennsylvania notables selected by Governor James Addams Beaver in October, 1887 to serve on a state Commission on Amended Orthography. Their report submitted in April 1889 hit all of the orthographical hot buttons. Focusing on governmental savings, the committee wittily called for removing the final "ugh" in "through" and the many similar words that are a particularly annoying feature of our tongue. They also maintained that the removal of silent "e" alone "would save four percent of all the letters on a common printed page..." There was high praise for "paternal" European governments, like Germany's, which had implemented some important spelling reforms despite opposition from Chancellor Otto Von Bismarck himself.

All of this meshed neatly with "Anglo-Saxonism." Channeling the shades of Webster, March and his acolytes tapped into an enthusiasm for Teutonic forebears that had long influenced many Americans' ideas about the roots of their language and culture. It also connected to a trend in American higher education to de-emphasize the Greek and Latin classics in favor of research and natural and social sciences, a shift very much inspired by German models of university teaching and curriculum. By 1893, Dr. March was hailing his nation's embrace of Anglo-Saxon language studies and culture.

There would be a darker side to this joyous paean to Anglo-Saxonism and Teutonic forebears – a racially-charged set of notions about language that was endemic in the spelling reform community and was hardly obscured by the volcano of hilarity that bubbled over

in 1906. Many of the same philologists, like March, who favored
linguistics over literature, and put the mechanics of language ahead
of its beauty and inspirational qualities, were also the most likely
to see English spelling as a curable nuisance, and spelling reform
as an appropriate tribute to America's master races – the Nordic,
Germanic, and Anglo-Saxon. Long before he became president or an
avowed spelling simplifier, Teddy Roosevelt was a leading advocate
of an America led by people like himself. He urged women from
proper racial pools to rear larger families, while also promoting strict
limits on immigration. By the time of the First World War, and beyond, this triumphalist subtext became an important, if less obvious,
problem for spelling reform and reformers in the twentieth century.
No such worries clouded the launch of March's Spelling Reform
League and its call for "reform by progressive steps." This initiative
asked adopters to "giv my name to be used in the list of advocates
of spelling reform, and agree to adopt for general use the simplified
spellings indicated by the number following my signature..."

These steps began by using the simplest spelling of common
words already approved by standard dictionaries, and escalated
from there. Step Two adopters agreed to use "thru" and "tho;" Step
Three added a promise to use "wisht, catalog, definit, hav, giv, liv,
gard, and ar." By Step Six, a truly dedicated adherent would be
using twenty-four rules jointly promulgated by the American and
English Philological Associations. Spelling pledges would be a key
feature in the failed 1906 effort to make spelling change a national
reality. In November of 1906, Brander Matthews claimed that his
Simplified Spelling Board had collected more than ten thousand
pledges, mainly from school teachers, professors, and "practical"
businessmen, despite the recent "defection" of Stanford University
president David Starr Jordan.

Matthews' plunge into orthographic controversy had begun in
July, 1892, when *Harper's New Monthly Magazine* ran his eight-page
article titled "As to 'American Spelling.'" He was born in 1852 in
New Orleans, where his father Edward, a sixth generation offspring

of Puritans, got rich in real estate. As secession loomed, the Matthews family relocated to New York City where James Brander Matthews was educated at Columbia College, then a rather sleepy and traditional school that focused on Greek, Latin, and rote memorization. Brander, as he was known was the opposite of sleepy, showing early talent for modern languages, drama, literary criticism, and cultural politics. So when Edward Matthews' dream of making his son a "professional millionaire" collapsed in the Panic of 1873, Brander was, on the whole, relieved.

By 1892, Matthews was already Theodore Roosevelt's good friend, and a professor of literature at Columbia. His witty *Harper's* essay was a brief for American cultural equality and literary independence. There was, Matthews wrote, a "tacit assumption that we Americans are outer [sic] barbarians, mere strangers, wickedly tampering with something which belongs to the British exclusively." At a time when both English-speaking nations were beginning the delicate process of revising international copyright laws, he noted, the London press greets "'American spelling'" as a "hideous monster" when, in fact, "it is idle to look for any logic in anything which has to do with modern English orthography on either side of the ocean."

Matthews argued a case for professional expertise, suggesting that British and American philologists were not just mere "men of letters" who "use words as the tools of their trade," but should be entrusted with the scientific reform of spelling. He hailed "irresistible forces" for uniformity, as evidenced by official language reform efforts not just in Germany, but in France, Italy, Spain, and Holland as well. None of those nations, he said, "stood half as much in need of the broom of reform as English..." He concluded by predicting that British assaults on American spelling would only make true reform more likely.

The dramatic rationalization and simplification of English spelling on scientific principles that Matthews foresaw in 1892, and by which he achieved both fame and failure in 1906, was not to be. On the tenth anniversary of Roosevelt's spelling directive, Matthews wrote an essay recalling the "unreasonable" and "rancorous" attacks on the former President, and tried to make the case that many newspapers and the influential National Education Association (NEA) were using "at least the Twelve Words" in greatest need of spelling reform. In their simplified form, these words were *program, catalog, decalog, prolog, pedagog, tho, altho, thoro, thoroly, thorofare, thru,* and *thruout.* Although *program* and *catalog* are now standard, and *thru* is a familiar informal usage, the rest of these twelve are pretty much resting in peace. His article was subtitled "Matthews Finds That the Public Has Had a Change of Heart and Is No Longer Contemptuously Hostile." By the time Brander Matthews died at age seventy-seven in 1929, after five years of declining health, his spelling crusade had become a fusty relic of an earlier era, and rated less than a sentence in the *New York Times'* otherwise long and appreciative obituary.

The idea of spelling reform was down, but by no means moribund. On Sunday, January 28, 1934, in the midst of the Great Depression, the *Chicago Tribune* announced on its front page that the paper had adopted "Saner Spelling of Many Words." The list was purposely limited, wrote James O'Donnell Bennett, so that readers would not be "irked by sudden sweeping changes" or the "immediate application of general rules, however logical..." The initial list offered twenty-four words, including *catalog, definitly, fantom,* and *hocky.* Only *catalog* survives.

Many *Trib* readers would have certainly recalled the Roosevelt list but only the oldest subscribers might have remembered that their newspaper had gone through this before. In September, 1879, Joseph Medill, a long-time spelling reform advocate and, from 1855 to his death in 1899 the Chicago newspaper's owner and publisher, launched what his staff called the "briefer" or "shorter" spelling, and dissenters dubbed "so-called spelling reform." For more than a year, *Tribune* columns were awash in applause and complaints, such as Mrs. M. F. P.'s who called the innovations "odious" and "a disgusting caricature." The newspaper was not merely bragging in early 1880 when it ran an article, datelined Boston, which called Chicago the "liveliest place in the whole country" for spelling reform. Medill's reform program was a relatively moderate one, focusing mainly on excising duplicate and silent letters. He apparently did not promote his own 1867 monograph in which he had proclaimed, "Lerning tu spel and red the Inglish langwaj iz the grat elementary task ov the pupol."

The newspaper's commitment to Medill's reforms faltered after his death until the challenge was taken up once more in 1934 by Col. Robert R. McCormick, Medill's grandson and heir, who briefly spelled his own name "M'Cormik." ("Why not M'Kormik?" one asks.) When James Wilson, Peoria's thirteen-year-old spelling champ, was interviewed in Chicago, en route to Washington, the *Trib* happily quoted him confiding, "I'm all for this new idea of simplified spelling...It wouldn't be hard to learn the whole spelling book if the words were simplified."

Less than a month after the initial launch, *Tribune* writer Bennett, who was a scholar and editor as well as a newspaperman, found himself trying to explain the logic behind the list of twenty-four, by now enriched with another eighteen respellings. Under the headline "*Tribune* Saner Spelling Draws Praise, Abuse," Bennett (whose own full name included four sets of double consonants) wrote, "On some days a chorus of praise. On some a clamor of protest. On others—both." By March, Bennett was evoking the abuse heaped on the first President Roosevelt as the *Tribune's* own list climbed to eighty words. After 1939, efforts to maintain or expand reformed spellings limped along, ending almost entirely four months after McCormick's death in 1955. Apparently, Chicago teachers were tired of arguing with students who used the *Tribune* to justify their spelling errors. Yet, when the paper reverted to standard spelling that August, few readers noticed the change. Spelling reform at Chicago's leading paper was officially laid to rest on September 29, 1975. As *Tribune* staff writer Eric Zorn wrote for the 150th anniversary year of his newspaper, "Though there was hubris and fatuousness in this, there was also something noble. The newspaper had an idea, thought it was good, gave it a shot, didn't hurt anybody...The 'Inglish langwaj' has recovered — and so have we."

Were all those generations of spelling reformers and simplifiers deluded? Their ranks included some of the most distinguished professors, philologists, philanthropists, phonographers, politicians, and thinkers on both sides of the Atlantic. Among them were dedicated teachers who struggled to force-feed spelling to children who might have been better served by more reading and less orthography.

But reformers stumbled in their enthusiasm and made excessive claims for the importance of their cause. Probably most damning and damaging was their seeming inability to agree on and follow through with a truly consistent system for representing the ever-more motley English language. Noah Webster's nemesis, Lyman Cobb, had been onto something when he attacked Webster's inconsistencies. Reformers who proposed to eliminate useless letters regularly failed to remove many of these from their own texts. Advocates of precise vowel sounds disagreed over how to represent each sound and became entangled in the difficulties of regional differences in pronunciation. Proponents of alphabetic tinkering confused students, annoyed lexicographers, and scared printers. English speakers who were excellent spellers – whether in the British, Canadian, Australian, or American way — maintained an irrational (or perhaps rational) fondness for the language's orthographic peculiarities. Those who could not spell very well at all found ways to minimize their discomfort as English, despite its very obvious flaws, became a second language to a large part of the world. To the extent spelling has changed – and it has – the process has been evolutionary rather than ordained or engineered.

Spelling reform, like Esperanto, still lives. Based in Britain, the Spelling Society, founded in 1908 as the Simplified Spelling Society is now open to members and supporters around the world via the Internet. Although its paid membership appears to be under a thousand, its sophisticated and regularly updated site is a trove of historical information and modern ideas, even though the words "reform" and "simple," no longer appear in the group's name.

Speaking in 2004 on his return from a visit to China during which he observed the struggles of Chinese students to acquire English, Spelling Society president John Wells held out hope for improvements in many aspects of English. "The utopian vision," said the Emeritus Professor of Phonics at University College London, "regards humankind as perfectible, and reforms as necessary for progress." The society, said Wells, is "firmly in the utopian camp, since we are committed to the view that illogical and inefficient setups - such as our traditional spelling system - can and should be changed." For its hundredth birthday in 2008, the society held a two-day conference at England's Coventry University titled "The Cost of Spelling." Francis March, Andrew Carnegie, and Brander Matthews might have felt right at home. In 2009, members mourned the death of Edward Rondthaler, a stalwart spelling reformer, frequent contributor, and accomplished and creative commercial printer who was born a year before Teddy Roosevelt's spelling fiasco. Rondthaler's death at age 104 left spelling, be it reformed or merely simplified, as a dream unfulfilled.

5 | *Bee Seasons*

During the Scripps National Spelling Bees of 2002 and 2008, dozens of contestants stopped air-writing words on their palms, or silently mouthing strings of letters, to line up for the autograph of Frank Neuhauser. Aged ninety-four at his 2008 appearance, he was a former Navy officer, retired patent attorney for General Electric, father of four, and Virginia's husband for sixty-three years. But none of that was as important as what he had done at the age of eleven. An only child from Louisville, Kentucky, educated at St. Brigid's School and drilled nightly by his father, Frank was the first champion in a contest that has since become the summit of spelling success in the U.S. and much of the English-speaking world. In 1925, he shook hands with President Calvin Coolidge and then bested eight other boys and girls when he correctly spelled "gladiolus." Awarded $500 in twenty-dollar gold pieces, Frank returned home to Louisville, where he was feted with a parade and a new bicycle. Said Neuhauser of his long-ago championship, "it was a lot easier back then. The words are, in my judgment, much more difficult. I'd never make it now."

He was not being falsely modest. The Bee's 2002 champion, thirteen-year-old Pratyush Buddiga of Colorado Springs, won the Bee and twelve thousand dollars by spelling "prospicience, defined as 'foresight.'" In 2008, champion Sameer Mishra of West Lafayette, Indiana, also thirteen, spelled "guerdon," defined as a "reward," for which he was awarded thirty-five thousand dollars. Each of these champions out-spelled more than two hundred "tween" rivals before national television audiences. The 2008 Bee even attracted the notice of the satirical tabloid, *The Onion*, which joked that Mishra had written the entire dictionary in his left palm, and said that Neuhauser "could be seen standing around asking if anyone wanted him to spell anything," only to be trampled by contestants in the "National Bullying Bee." (Neuhauser died at age 97 in March 2011.)

It was obvious to press and public that both recent champions had names and backgrounds marking each as an outsider. Buddiga was born in New Zealand to parents from India; both Mishra, and his sister Shruti, a three-time Bee contestant who coached him to victory, were born in the U.S. to Indian parents. Indeed, between 1985 when Balu Natarajan, the Chicago-born son of Indian speakers of English and Tamil, won the Bee, eleven others with links to the Indian subcontinent had become champions as of 2012 and growing numbers of contestants from other non-U.S and non-English-speaking backgrounds were regularly excelling.

Such changes to an institution as patriotic as apple pie or American spelling were not entirely new. In 1915, Fuyuko Fukai, a fourteen-year-old Oregon girl of Japanese descent, won a local spelling bee, an event shocking enough to draw newspaper attention. A continent away, a *New York Times* writer called this "A Victory for the Japanese" that had humiliated her native-born rivals and seemed to justify "Japanese unpopularity" on the West Coast. But, he added, "that the little alien should have mastered all the mysteries, all the wild absurdities and inconsistencies of English spelling is a remarkable feat."

A 1920 Carnegie Foundation study was more sympathetic to immigrants' educational struggles, suggesting that the foreign-born, especially adults and older children, needed only to learn to "spell a few words well," just enough to speak and read English without mastering thousands of common words. In a more welcoming acknowledgement of first and second generation spelling accomplishment, the *Washington Post* and other newspapers at the 1929 National Bee noted the participation of young spellers of the French, Hebrew, Italian, Polish, Czech, and, yes, even Japanese extraction, making the Bee "not unlike a list of the delegates at a League of Nations conference."

In recent years, the National Bee has welcomed the participation of young Americans abroad, and has encouraged sponsored English-speakers from China, South Korea, Ghana, New Zealand, and some Pacific and Caribbean island nations with U.S. ties to participate. In 1998, Jody-Anne Maxwell, a twelve-year-old Jamaican, became the national Bee's first black and first non-U.S. champion. This breakthrough was clouded for more than a year by a threat of disqualification for failing to meet Bee rules, but ended happily when the *Gleaner* newspaper, for forty years sponsor of Jamaica's National Children's Own Spelling Bee, was welcomed back to the Scripps Bee.

Since 2005, Canadian media conglomerate, CanWest, in partnership with Air Canada and the nation's egg farmers, has crowned a CanSpell national champion in Ottawa, and sends scores of regional champs to compete in Washington. Francophones can participate, but only in English. In addition to *Webster's Third New International Dictionary of the English Language, Unabridged,* the *Canadian Oxford Dictionary* is an official spelling source. Many Americanisms, such as *neighbor* as an alternate to *neighbour* or *honor* for *honour*, are allowed. In both 2006 and 2007, spellers from Alberta came in second in Washington.

Long before geographical or cultural "outsiders" excelled in America's spelling contests, the fundamental peculiarity of competitive spelling and the odd ardor of its disciples had been widely noted, attracting both ridicule and awe. A nineteenth-century boy who aspired to be a top-notch speller was viewed as an annoying "Memorus Wordus" or a stoop-shouldered prig, while girls were mocked for parading their often superior spelling abilities. New York newspaper publisher and Republican politician Horace Greeley, born into a poor New England farm family in 1811, was a master speller by age four who "wept bitterly" when he lost a match, possibly for the first and last time. Years later he made fun of his own spelling obsession, saying it was "my forte, as is natural for a child of tenacious memory and no judgment." He also pled guilty to "spelling well enough to be 'head' among thirty or forty numskulls, whose incapability of learning to spell is even now a puzzle to me..." Greeley's spelling correctness likely struck fear into careless *Tribune* writers and might have served him very well indeed in a national spelling contest, but he died in 1872, weeks after his unsuccessful presidential campaign. So famed was Greeley's precocious spelling ability that it was mentioned at length in his *New York Times* obituary.

The nation's centennial decade would usher in both a season of spelling bee mania and an upsurge of interest in spelling reform and simplification. While bee fanatics celebrated or even fetishized the difficulties of English, the equally dedicated simplifiers had very different prescriptions for the rigors and annoyances of American spelling. Fueled largely by the popularity of Edward Eggleston's best-selling *Hoosier Schoolmaster*, the 1870's Bee boom spawned matches testing both school children and adults, and accompanied by musical tributes. In 1875 alone, from Cincinnati came Berthould Touris' "Spelling Match Waltz;" from Philadelphia, the prolific composer Edward Mack's "Spelling Bee March for Piano," and, from Boston, "respectfully dedicated to all the bad spellers," J. W. Turner's "The Spelling Match," a waltz for piano and voice.

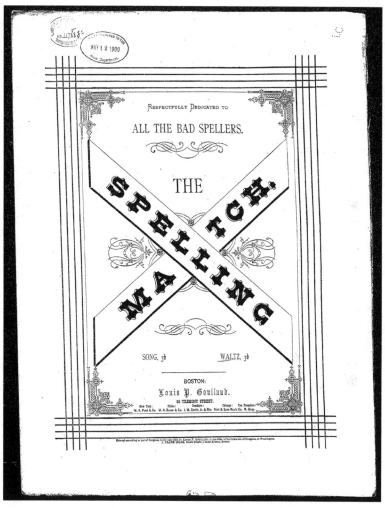

A Matchless Spelling Match

Serious competition required lists of impressively tricky words. Speller authors were ready to oblige. In 1869, Nathaniel P. Henderson, a New York City grammar school teacher, scored with his *Henderson's Test Words in English Orthography*, a book that remained popular, especially in New York schools, until at least 1895. More than half of his speller's 105 pages consisted of words of spelling-bee caliber, briskly defined but presented in no discernible order or pattern. Aimed at students who would be today's equivalent of college-bound high schoolers, Henderson's list began with "vicissitude," followed by "embassador" (now considered an archaic spelling) and "embarrassment." "Guerdon," the very word that won the 2008 National Spelling Bee, appeared sixty daunting pages later.

Bret Harte, the Albany, New York-born author who reinvented himself as an interpreter of the West, was at the height of his fame when his humorous poem, "The Spelling Bee at Angels," appeared in *Scribner's Monthly* in 1878. The grizzled and presumably dangerous denizens of a California mining camp become quivering wrecks as they attempt "a new game down in Frisco, thet ez far ez I kin see/ Beats euchre, poker and van-toon, they calls the 'Spellin' Bee.'" Incited by Lenny, a supposed schoolmaster who proffers such words as "phthisis," "parallel," "gneiss," and "eider-duck," a huge brawl ensues:

> ...here got up Three-fingered Jack and locked the door and yelled: /
> 'No, not one mother's son goes out till that thar word is spelled!'/
> But while the words were on his lips, he groaned and sank in pain,/
> And sank with Webster on his chest, and Worcester on his brain...

Harte's clever melding of high and low culture and dialect surely brought smiles to urbane *Scribner's* readers; today, his scenes of gladiatorial spelling, at once juvenile and dangerous, mesh nicely with the defining tropes of the modern spelling bee: fear, pride, determination, with undertones of adolescent angst.

Although spelling bee enthusiasm diminished after the 1870s, and Edward Eggleston died in 1902, the next century offered new reasons to highlight the educational importance of spelling. Enjoying what would prove to be the zenith of their influence, the nation's newspapers had stepped up almost to a man to deplore President Roosevelt's unsuccessful 1906 experiment in spelling reform. During and after World War I, many papers also gave voice to unions, educators, and nativists concerned that immigration might be diluting American spelling along with other founding values. Finding "Few Good Spellers," attributed to the failures of modern education and the lure of the movies, the *Indianapolis News* in late 1918 suggested that a spelling match revival "might produce a great deal of good." It would take another seven years before novice publisher Robert Worth Bingham, a proponent of woman suffrage, supporter of the League of Nations, ally of President Franklin D. Roosevelt, and defender of Darwinism, used his *Louisville Courier-Journal* to institutionalize a national spelling contest that endures today.

Bingham was born in North Carolina in 1871 into a family that had owned slaves and likely had links to the Ku Klux Klan. University-educated, Bingham in his twenties taught Latin and Greek at the Bingham School, a rigorous academy for young white men founded by his grandfather before the war. Married to a Louisvillian heiress, he became a local eminence in his adopted city as an influential lawyer and judge. In 1918, he took ownership of the city's leading newspaper, later launching Kentucky's first radio station, WHAS, which would soon broadcast local spelling contests.

Fourteen years later, Douglas D. Cornette, the *Courier-Journal's* spelling bee reporter and director, explained that the Bee had begun, "as a program to take an interest in the usually dull subject of spelling." He added, "The group at which the spelling bee aims is not the group of brilliant children who are naturally good spellers..." but was meant rather to inspire better spelling "among the poorer pupils." Worthy goal though this was, Cornette's modest proposal was already being overtaken by more "extreme" spelling contests.

The new Bee was a success. Although only nine spellers engaged in orthographical (or more correctly, orthoepical) combat in the first Washington Bee in June, 1925, the President took notice and an

Capitol Spellers and Their Fans

estimated two million children competed in local and state contests. In 1926, just eight competed, but by 1928, twenty-three finalists, sixteen girls and seven boys, took part. From the beginning, the Bee cultivated heartland values that struck some of the nation's larger newspapers as unfashionably quaint. A *New York Times* editorial in 1939 called the Bee revival "depressing" and mocked that year's winning word, *canonical,* while blaming teachers and the popular new Dictaphone recording device for the poor state of genuine spelling accomplishment. A Louisville reader with ties to his local newspaper took umbrage. For fifteen years, wrote Carlile Crutcher, the *Courier-Journal* had poured resources and enthusiasm into the cause of better spelling, while the *Times* and far too many other newspapers "have refused to assist us in dramatizing spelling and making it interesting" Some newspapers, he added, "have been downright insulting." New York's most prestigious paper never did answer Crutcher's call but the tabloid *New York Daily News* eventually became a Bee sponsor.

Sponsors in 1928 included the *Detroit News*, which had launched its own Bee in 1922, the *Buffalo Evening News*, and newspapers in Des Moines, Indianapolis, Milwaukee, Worcester, Massachusetts, Akron and Youngstown, Ohio, and New Britain and Bridgeport, Connecticut. Betty Robinson, representing the South Bend, Indiana *News-Times*, won the thousand dollar prize. In 1939's "League of Nations" bee, just twenty-one students, seventeen girls and four boys, took part. The lingering Depression likely took a toll; 1939 champion, Elizabeth Ann Rice of Worcester, Massachusetts, took home $500, half the 1928 prize. The newspaper company now known as Scripps would acquire rights to the national spelling bee three years after Robert Bingham's death in December, 1937. During the war years of 1943, '44, and '45 no Bees were held.

The Binghams' newspapers had offered many Kentucky children elaborate and well-publicized opportunities for spelling success. Identical spelling contests were administered in the months before the national bee, one for public school children and the other for youngsters, such as Frank Neuhauser of St. Brigid's, who learned their spelling in religious schools. But there would be no opportunity for a new Marie Bolden to spell her way to national acclaim. Louisville was then a city in which African-Americans could vote, but their children were sent to segregated schools. The newspaper, for all its progressivism, remained paternalistic on issues of race. For years, publisher Barry Bingham Sr. who took over when his father Robert was named ambassador to Britain, presented winning white spellers with the collected editorials of the late Henry Watterson, the Kentucky Colonel who was the newspaper's founding publisher. During Roosevelt's 1906 spelling controversy, Watterson had happily joined in the merriment on August 25, suggesting that the President spell his name "Rucevelt...the first silabel riming with goose." Watterson's racial views, though moderate in this era of Ku Klux Klan resurgence, can be glimpsed in his nickname, "Marse (as in Master) Henry."

African-American spellers were not entirely ignored in Louisville. A polite but brief 1941 *C-J* article included a photograph of thirteen-year-old eighth-grader Althea Williams who had bested twenty-four other black youngsters in Jefferson County's Negro Spelling Match. Williams' win entitled her to compete that April in the Kentucky Negro State Spelling Bee. African-Americans and other minority spellers, including a number of blind children, apparently got closer to Bee competition. In 1930, Vernon Jack, of the Tuscarora tribe was the Niagara County champion. In 1938, local champions representing Buffalo and eight Western New York counties included eighth grader Wendell E. Gault of Olean, "a Negro pupil," and fifteen year old Franklin Bennett from the Cattaraugus Tuscarora reservation who came in third. By 1947, African-American Donna Steed, whose race was not singled out for comment, was the City of Buffalo champion. Not until the Sixties did the fairness of Bee racial policies become overtly but briefly contentious.

A more riveting issue for newspaper sponsors and the public at large was the apparent dominance of girl spellers. In 1875, a big city reporter called spelling matches "an epidemic" and "rural" amusement, and heaped scorn on a "young lady" for misspelling the word "khan." He suggested that mankind (if not woman-kind) would be far better served had she baked a cake for her future husband instead of trying to win one in a spelling bee. By the time bees were institutionalized in the 1920s, "spelling wars of the sexes" might be enjoyed as jolly, even romantic, rivalries, ala Eggleston, or portend the collapse of both muscular Americanism and the primacy of male erudition. In the Bee's earliest years, both a National Champion Boy Speller and National Champion Girl Speller were crowned in Washington. Despite much evidence of female spelling prowess, a promotional booklet from the early 1930s assumed that the speller "who defeats all other finalists," thereby becoming overall champion, would be a "he."

In each bee season from 1938 to 1942, the largest *Courier-Journal* headlines heralded boys' spelling achievements. When Jimmy Hill and Morton Tenenbaum slugged it out in 1938, it was described as a "word battle such as never has been seen before in Louisville's Public School spelling bee...a series of thrills..." (Jimmy, the younger boy, won). Kenneth Toomey of rural Garrard County, a three-time runner-up in the state bee, was billed as a great boy hope who would "give the girls a real spelling lesson" when he qualified for a fourth time in 1940. A month later second-time contender Bobby Hurst was singled out as bearer of the "pleasing" news that "an unusual number of boys placed high" in Louisville's public school qualifying bee. Days later, a seventh-grade boy outspelled "Smart Girls" to win the county parochial title.

For All Who Never "One" a Bee

In 1941, William Porter, a "blond, sturdily built" seventh grader from Holy Name School, "rippled through a series of tongue-twisting words with the coolness and finesse of a Notre Dame quarterback..." At the Kentucky state bee that May, Porter came in fifth, misspelling the word "pirouette," a rather less manly maneuver. The better news was that Billy Styles from Union County was headed to Washington after becoming the first boy in eight years to represent Kentucky.

For both girls and boys the actual experience of competitive spelling was, and is, deeply personal and altogether too easy to caricature, especially because contestants are already struggling with all the many ills and insults that adolescence confers on children between the ages of nine and fifteen — prime time for both spelling excellence and painful insecurity. Middle school is a notorious social minefield. Orthodontic appliances abound. That girls of that age group tend to be physically more mature than boys assures that many girl spellers will tower over boys with squeaky voices.

To ease the inevitable anxiety, there are good luck talismans – a favorite bracelet, a lucky article of clothing, a beloved doll or action figure, an idiosyncratic mantra for tackling the word at hand. In 1941, Louisville contestant Martha Harmon, who had been dealt the number thirteen in an early round, insisted on keeping her "bad omen" once it brought her success. In 1971, a politically-polarized year, New York City co-champion Marcie S. Gitlin managed to make a statement and allay nerves by wearing a "funky" hat adorned with a peace symbol to a spellers' tea hosted by First Lady Pat Nixon. No amount of spelling practice can inoculate young competitors from tripping up on words that they have come to know better than their own names. Especially in the early rounds, accomplished spellers seem about as likely as the unprepared to bungle some easy words. Gitlin was relaxed enough to come in seventh among seventy-seven spellers. The word she missed: *chalazion*, a type of eye tumor.

Since the 1990s, when Scripps's long-running spelling show achieved mass market attention, books, documentaries, plays, and feature films have probed the Bee phenomenon. The most satisfying as literature is certainly *Bee Season*, Myla Goldberg's 2000 novel, later made into a 2005 film starring Richard Gere and Juliette Binoche as the parents, and newcomer Flora Cross as budding speller Eliza Naumann. (Oddly, the first language of both Binoche and Cross is French). Eliza is the designated underachiever in her erudite but deeply unhappy Jewish family until, in fifth grade, she suddenly and almost magically manifests a talent for spelling. Competing in the Norristown *Times-Herald* bee in southeastern Pennsylvania, Eliza pays little attention to insincere assertions that everyone is a winner upholding a great American tradition. Instead, she enters into a mystical language experience, unmoored from dictionaries, word lists, or even competitors:

> ...the words are there, radiant as neon. She hears the word and suddenly it is inside her head, translated from sound to physical form. Sometimes the letters need a moment to arrange themselves behind her closed eyes. An E will replace an I, a consonant will double....Eliza wins the district bee with VACUOUS.

The mediocre little sister is suddenly a family star. *I am the best speller at the dinner table,* she tells herself. Her head "becomes an ocean of consonants and vowels, swirling and crashing in huge waves of letters until the word she wants begins to rise to the surface." At the state finals in Philadelphia's old hockey arena, "A lot of time is spent raising and lowering the mike stand between contestants who have hit puberty and those still waiting to grow." Eliza spells with her eyes closed, seeing letters on her own internal screen. The contest becomes a duel between Eliza and an equally short Pakistani boy. She wins at last, eyes closed, by spelling *eyrir,* a unit of Icelandic currency and a word she has never before seen, heard, nor spelled.

Saul, Eliza's distant and distracted father, reinvents himself as her greatest fan, even buying his daughter an expensive dictionary. She yields to his belated enthusiasm when she discovers that dictionary pages look very much like the visions she has seen behind closed eyes. Soon father and daughter are drilling almost forty hours a week in preparation for the National Bee, both of them ignoring her mother, a lawyer turned kleptomaniac, and older brother who has joined a Hari Krishna-like sect.

In Washington, Eliza allows herself to imagine winning. But, as one of seventeen spellers still "alive," she misspells *duvetyn,* a twilled fabric. In the Bee's "Comfort Room" she is consoled with cookies and juice, like a spent blood donor. For months she will indulge an obsession to spell every interesting word she sees or hears, and accepts her father's plan for a second run at the national Bee. This effort will include word study based on the obscure writings of a proscribed Jewish mystic. But as her father looks on confidently, Eliza instead stands up at her local school bee, which for her is a baby step on the road back to Washington, and claims her independence by intentionally misspelling "origami," ending it with a *y*.

In Goldberg's intricate drama, a family's actions, words, and feelings, some of them "spelled" right and others badly mangled or unspoken, cause both pain and truth to emerge. *Akeelah and the Bee,* a 2006 film, shares with *Bee Season* the importance of family engagement, but here the role of spelling is less metaphorical and more inspirational, celebrating the educational potential of African-American children and the communities that can nurture or stymie them.

Eleven-year-old Akeelah (played by Keke Palmer) lives with her widowed mother (Angela Bassett) in South Central Los Angeles' Crenshaw district. Initially reluctant to be "special" and lacking her frazzled mother's support, Akeelah forges a consent form and is soon taken on by Dr. Joshua Larabee (Laurence Fishburne) an English professor and former Bee contestant who was "dinged" in the third round and has suffered his own experiences of loss and doubt. Like Saul in *Bee Season*, Larabee encourages his pupil to experience what here might be called the Zen of spelling, rather than rote memorization of champion word lists. As Akeelah surmounts her fear of becoming a "brainiac," she heads to Washington, energizing her community and recovering her spelling rhythm by jumping rope. Akeelah also becomes aware of the very different lives of spellers from more privileged or parentally-involved backgrounds as she comes very close to winning.

Both of these fictional accounts pale before the real-life drama of *Spellbound,* director Jeffery Blitz's documentary of the seventy-second National Bee of 1999, released in 2002. It follows eight contestants, some of them repeating regional champs, to Washington. Sensitively tuned by region, socioeconomic status, parental involvement, and schoolmate interaction, *Spellbound* does not entirely avoid clichés about the kinds of kids, parents, and teachers who think spelling is important (or at least a great way to stand out). But it does allow the individuality of this motley crew of young adolescents to emerge. There are the "foreigners," including a Texas girl, Angela, whose father once illegally entered the U. S. from Mexico and still speaks no English. There is Neil from California whose successful Indian father seeks to guarantee his son's championship by endless word drills, employing four paid coaches, each expert in a different European language. The eventual winner, Nupur Lala of Tampa, is a second-time competitor and daughter of Indian parents who seem much more relaxed than Neil's. As she heads to the Bee, the local Hooters Restaurant proudly proffers "Congradulations" on its outdoor billboard.

The "Americans" are equally diverse. Ashley has the shortest physical journey but a longer psychic one: she lives in an African-American neighborhood that few Washington tourists ever see. Unlike the fictional Akeelah, Ashley knows that her mother is immensely proud of her. Living in rural Missouri, where his parents raise peacocks and his father teaches remedial classes, Ted uses his sports prowess to neutralize an extensive vocabulary that stumps most of his fellow students. April's father owns the Easy Street Pub in a Connecticut town where asbestos was once a linchpin of the economy. Despite her shyness, braces, and pessimism, a word she uses often, April makes it to the final four. Northern New Jersey twelve-year-old Harry is one of those endearingly prepubescent boys with braces and an inexhaustible fund of jokes and bits that almost mask his determination to do well. Emily, appearing for a third and final time, hails from a wealthy New Haven family who brought their au pair to previous bees. "I am not in *love* with spelling," she confides. Having made it into the "ESPN" round, where Bee contestants appear live on television, she seems quite happy to be "dinged" soon after. In a thoughtful critique of Spellbound, Scott Hanes, a student at the University of Washington, questioned the validity of equating spelling bee success with the presumed successes of American education more generally and the American Dream more globally, thereby sentimentalizing issues in need of more rigorous analysis. In fact, he observed, participants already blessed with ample resources of both money and social capital remain the most likely to succeed in life, even if they do not win the spelling bee.

In comparison to *Spellbound*, the hit musical, *The Twenty-Fifth Annual Putnam County Spelling Bee* is a throwback to the misfit-geek model: an often corny cross between Eggleston's Hoosiers and the documentary's more comical moments. It is a lampoon with heart, or as one critic has called it, a *"Chorus Line* with pimples" that celebrates "that most revered of American virtues, the will to victory." First staged in 2004 and successfully transplanted to Broadway in 2005, *Putnam County* won two Tony awards and has become a spelling staple.

As Mark Twain once remarked more seriously, "Some people have an idea that correct spelling can be taught – and taught to anybody. That is a mistake. The spelling faculty is born in a man, like poetry, music, and art. It's a gift, a talent." There are 114,000 words in the unabridged dictionary, he observed, but only a few exceptionally endowed spellers can "see a word once in print and it is forever photographed upon their memory." (The Merriam-Webster dictionary used at the national Bee currently boasts four hundred seventy thousand entries).

Despite Twain's cautionary remarks, competitive adult bees that run the gamut from grim intensity to outright burlesque are broadly popular. Business and civic groups often use bee formats to enliven fundraising for local causes. There have been bees for word hipsters, including at least two "Ersatz Spelling Bees" in the 1990s, each a "festival of orthography" for some of New York City's more prominent writers, editors, and wordsmiths. It was reported in 2005 that fiercely competitive twenty- and thirty-somethings were regularly gathering in a shabby-chic Williamsburg, Brooklyn bar for rounds of spelling and beer. A "National Adult Spelling Bee" offering a thousand dollar first prize held its fifth contest in 2010. It was conceived by Long Beach, California event promoter Justin Rudd, whose other enterprises included beauty contests and dog parks. In February 2004, a television mini-series, "The Great American Celebrity Spelling Bee," assembled a motley throng of D-list celebrities, from Alice Cooper to Alan Thicke, all apparently so spelling-challenged that they needed a recent national bee finalist to show them the way.

Such semi-faux spelling matches haves their own long history, including a 1934 benefit Bee in Chicago's Hotel LaSalle. Armed with eighth-grade spellers, forty Lions club members, all distinguished local business and professional men, proceeded to misspell virtually every word, from "pronunciation" to "pharmacopoeia." It helps to know that each misspelled word added fifty cents to a Christmas charity fund. Only a Scrooge would try to spell each word right. The *Chicago Tribune* hailed the Lions' bee. Months earlier the *Trib*, long an outspoken advocate of simpler spellings, had introduced many of them in the daily paper. "As for the Lion who missed on a monstrosity like pharmacopoeia, he is a rebel we applaud," the paper editorialized a few days later.

Considerably more serious is the AARP National Spelling Bee that offers prizes and is sponsored by the nation's largest retiree organization and held each June since 1996 in Cheyenne, Wyoming. The overt goal is to keep aging brains agile; a bonus is the chance to "showcase a lifetime of knowledge... celebrate...years of experience" and possibly even learn "how to twitter during the spelling bee." Competitors must be at least fifty. Like the National Bee in more recent years, the AARP Bee uses a written spelling test to winnow the number of oral contestants. Participants must correctly write seventy-eight of a hundred words to take part in the oral rounds. The 2009 winner, Michael Petrina Jr., sixty-four, of Arlington, Virginia cut his teeth on the 1958 National Bee.

The 2008 winner, fifty-six year-old Larry Grossman, a North Dakota high school math teacher, wrote after his triumph that he had long regretted missing out on the Scripps Bee. Preparing for his victory, Grossman did what any speller worth his or her salt would do. He bought an updated dictionary, compiled lists of unfamiliar words, and even recorded them on CDs. "Jump at the chance," he urged other seniors. "Why should you let just the young kids have all the fun?" Well before the modern bee era, educators, journalists, linguists, spelling reformers, and the general public were already asking whether competitive spellers were smug geniuses, over-trained parrots, or something in between. In 1970, the *Buffalo Evening News* took a stab at this issue in an article headlined "Over the Years, Champion Spellers Have Been Winners in Life Too."

In the absence of a comprehensive study, interesting nuggets can also be gleaned from *How to Spell Like a Champ*, an official Scripps National Bee manual for aspiring super-spellers. Although poets, journalists, humanities professors, and copy editors have all appeared over the years, by far the most consistent calling among former spelling champs seems to be the medical profession. Balu Natarajan, the 1985 champion who was the first youth of Indian descent to win, is a sports physician in his native Chicago; 1999 champion Nupur Lala, featured in *Spellbound*, went on to the University of Michigan for a degree in biochemistry. This apparent trend emerged long before Indian contestants and national television transformed the National Bee. Of the twenty-one winners since 1941, highlighted in *How to Spell Like a Champ*, eleven chose medicine and allied professions. Four were involved in writing or media occupations including 1973 winner Barrie Trinkle, co-author of the *Champ* book. There were also two attorneys and, at one each, a third-grade teacher, an engineer, a business woman, and Paige Pipkin Kimble, the 1981 champion who became the Scripps Bee director a decade later. One now-famous Bee contender was "dinged" in the 1964 championship. Eleven-year-old South Carolinian Ben S. Bernanke came in twenty-sixth when he misspelled *edelweiss*. As he neared confirmation as chairman of the Federal Reserve Board forty-one years later, Bernanke's spelling prowess appeared in the headline of a *Washington Post* profile.

Asked if correct spelling really matters, Dr. Natarajan, the 1985 spelling champion, had this to say:

> When I write I should use proper grammar and spell correctly....When I take care of patients in my practice, I should follow fundamentals and focus on that patient, without distraction and without bias. Life seems to be better when we do things correctly. It usually takes longer to do so and occasionally will cost us money, but I think it's the right way to live.

In 2013 the National Bee added a test meant to minimize rote memorization and possibly favor meaning over mere words.

As spelling reform proceeds, or not, at a glacial pace, the annual celebration of our wonderfully peculiar language, as enshrined in the Bee process, is both endearing and threatening. Despite years of complaints, neither non-English words nor non-traditional contestants materially threaten the Bee heritage. The greatest challenges to the current American Spelling Bee system appear to be two: the creation of higher tech spelling study materials that might give special advantages to some contestants, and the difficulty of assuring broad participation as newspapers, so long at the proudly beating heart of the Bee tradition, investigate new business models or simply and sadly disappear.

6 | *Spelling is Dead.*
| *Long Live Spelling!*

On a mild December day at Lakeland Elementary School in mid-Michigan, more than two dozen second-graders are buzzing about amid low tables. Halfway through the school year, they know the drill. It is time for their daily three-hour exposure to what the state education department calls "balanced literacy." Their teacher, a veteran of eleven years, does not merely stand in front of her class, but circulates, encourages, prods, and mediates. Each school day, a quarter of the class will focus on spelling for twenty minutes, while other students write in their journals, improve their penmanship, or read from a selection of books scattered about the room and ranging in difficulty from "emergent" to "fluent." When twenty minutes are up, each group migrates to another language "pod." Assisted by their teacher and an aide, every child is working on literacy for ninety minutes, but few are on the same page.

These young spellers encounter an array of strategies for

improving and expanding their ability. "Rainbow Words" use different colors to represent different letters. An exercise called "Brain and Fold" encourages students to examine a word, fold their paper over, and then try to spell it without looking. Sometimes, spellers vie to alphabetize a series of words. One little girl sits with the teacher, struggling mightily to connect images of apples to letters she does not seem to recognize. The good spellers in this busy classroom already know who they are. One eager boy says he could already spell "because" when he was in Kindergarten. A poised girl reports that "hypothesis" is the hardest word she has spelled so far, and then she aces "Mississippi." Many others are less enthusiastic. A particularly feisty boy asked if he spells well says, "Not really. I don't like spelling. I want it to be done." Another says he is beginning to like spelling but prefers math and gym. There are no spelling bees in elementary classrooms – too much potential for public embarrassment. And, since 2007, Michigan public elementary schools no longer provide a stand-alone grade for the spelling component of the literacy program.

These Michigan teachers, and many others across the United States, find themselves on spelling's front lines, even though this legendary subject, at least in theory, now takes a back seat. Here and elsewhere, spelling's apparent demotion has made many uneasy. Spelling drills are still such a time-honored marker of children's educational progress, and a straightforward way for parents to help their children – and recall their own youthful struggles -- that many feel disappointed or even angry.

Although Michigan's education department has reduced spelling's prominence in the curriculum, Pinckney Community Schools teachers have headed in a different direction. Using a variety of modern spelling texts, workbooks, and readers, they have been trying instead to emphasize spelling improvement. It has not been easy. Their students' language skills, these educators say, remain wildly variable. Kindergarten is not mandatory in this state so many first graders arrive unable to spell their own names. The recent popularity, here as elsewhere, of fancifully-spelled or unique names rarely makes their owners better spellers. By second grade, some children are clearly "getting it," but most are not or at least not yet. If a student is just not ready to engage, repetition and drill are of little use, the teachers report. Even in the third and fourth grades, some children are still using only consonants, ignoring the trickster vowels, those damnable five "harlequins" that Horace Mann scorned more than a century ago. Several teachers report that excellent spellers remain a tiny minority, perhaps just five students in a class of twenty-eight. Most but not all will improve with age, but there are few penalties for invented or just plain bad spelling, as long as the writer's intentions can be discerned. For quite a few high school juniors, only when they encounter the essay portion of their Michigan Merit Exams, during which spell-checkers are deactivated, are the depths of their spelling abyss revealed. Such embarrassment may soon be obsolete. In 2011, Oregon's Department of Education began allowing spell-checkers as an optional tool for middle and high schoolers taking standardized state exams.

To believe that Americans' spelling abilities have declined, and, more importantly, that it truly matters, is an ideological struggle for our times that Noah Webster might have savored. Every generation since has been certain that its members spelled better than their children, or, at the very least, tried harder. Although there is no conclusive evidence that today's adults spell worse than their forebears, more people than ever before are now writing, generating oceans of misspelled words. Thanks in part to new technologies that broadcast writing far beyond the older media of books, magazines, and newspapers, we are all writers now, and writing, unlike speaking, entails spelling. Even as we marvel at those talented youngsters who can conjure fantastic words out of thin air in a high stakes parlor game called the National Spelling Bee, daily written spelling is at the center of our modern spelling malaise.

For almost two centuries, spelling was the tail that wagged the educational dog. It is no wonder, then, that an upsurge of new teaching regimens conceived in the 1930s and fully ripened in the early 1970s, have made many feel uneasy. Once upon a time, spelling was the magic key to unlock literacy; nowadays it often seems an afterthought or even a hindrance. Amid gaudy and bewildering arrays of textbooks, workbooks, self-help games, and electronic devices, one thing seems clear. Spelling is still a pedagogical and sociological fault line and in America, latter-day adherents of Webster and Horace Mann are still duking it out.

In 1997, Elaine Woo, an education writer at the *Los Angeles Times*, wrote a lengthy article replete with (intentional) spelling errors and high indignation. Her opening line: "How do you spell failure?" She focused on dreadful spelling by eighth graders in California. The Golden State, she claimed, had become the nation's poster child for spelling incompetence when state educators decided a decade earlier to "largely abandon...spelling instruction." It did not help that so-called Ebonics, a vernacular used by some young African-Americans, ignited a huge controversy in Oakland, California around the same time. The supposed villains were not just Californians, but "as California went whole hog for 'whole language'" so, apparently, went the nation. As Woo's article put it, "Du we hav a problum hear?" The answer was "yes."

The "problum" was and is, older and more tenacious than many realize. Rudolf Flesch, a World War II refugee from Austria, in 1955 riled American educators and energized parents with his passionate indictment of established mid-century teaching methods. His bestseller, *Why Johnny Can't Read*, attributed the demise of language skills, including spelling, to an obscure upstate New York village schoolmaster named John Russell Webb who in 1846 introduced his "new word method" after helping a little girl connect the word "cow" to the animal her father was milking. Flesch scorned such accidental breakthroughs and blamed weak-kneed teachers of the Thirties whom, he said, felt sorry for their students' "heartless drudgery." He also complained that such texts as the monotonous Fifties favorite, "Dick and Jane," only encouraged those who wanted to abandon the alphabet and phonics in favor of a "look-say" method of guessing, memorization, and feel-good exercises. Flesch said of his "Johnnys, "They can't read; they can't spell. Not only that, they can't even learn how to spell properly because they have been equipped with mental habits that are almost impossible to break..." His own seventy-two steps to reading success were reminiscent of Webster's *Blue-Backs*, only better organized.

Teach Your Children LOL

Clashes begun in the nineteenth and twentieth centuries still inform the twenty-first. In a nation in which childhood education – be it public or private, magnet, religious, or chartered -- is both a huge industry and a deeply ideological cause, it is not surprising that both prescriptivists and pragmatists battle over spelling and its related literacy skills. To simplify drastically, the spelling education imbroglio boils down to a choice: shall we ply children with honey, or make them take a sterner medicine? The first option, aka whole language (or what Flesch called "word-guessing) ingratiates itself with children and many teachers by letting them express themselves well before they can reliably wield the tools of correct expression. The second path, aka phonics, promises children who practice obediently that they will soon be deemed worthy to express themselves. Each of these learning schemes can succeed; both can and do also fail. As literacy expert E. Jennifer Monaghan commented in 1996 as California's controversies reached full bloom, panicky responses to children's literacy failings could use a good dose of historical context. She further suggested that this perceived national literacy panic was most likely to benefit textbook authors and publishers, not parents and teachers.

Teaching spelling, by any method and to any age group, is far from easy. English has rules but these are riddled with exceptions and special cases that are often more confusing than enlightening. One spelling "tool-kit" from 1976 included "rules and patterns involving short vowel sounds." Teachers are reminded that, "The student must be made aware that whenever he hears a short vowel sound, he should be ready to 'think...'" because "Something special is apt to happen." What actually ensues is a list of exceptions to virtually each newly introduced rule. A sample rule: "In a one syllable word, double the final *f, l, s,* and *z* after a single vowel." The examples include *tell, miss, buzz,* and *roll.* But a host of exceptions include *if, gas, this, us, yes,* and *bus.* And there is more: "Final *s* sounded as *z* is never doubled, as in *as, was, has,* and *his.*" In other words, many words that children regularly use are in fact spelling landmines. Learning to spell and teaching others to spell remain huge challenges for literacy instructors and students of every stripe.

Those who seek more useful spelling rules or genuine, consistent, and widely-accepted reforms are also likely to be disappointed. In June, 2009, Britons awoke to learn that a "Support for Spelling" initiative prepared by a government agency was scrapping the mantra "*i* before *e* except after *c,*" a rule, venerated by generations of English spellers worldwide. This rule, said the authors "is not worth teaching" because its exceptions far outstrip its usefulness." Which is true, but the ensuing hubbub convincingly shows this "rule" to be virtually the only one anyone has ever remembered and actually used. Author Judy Parkinson used this opportunity to remind the public that her 2008 book, *I Before E (Except after C)* had sold 450,000 copies in the UK alone. By happy or unhappy coincidence, this spelling thunderbolt hit just as the *Times* of London was preparing to host Britain's first-ever spelling bee. If pages of instructions that rarely work, or a few bromides that do, cannot teach spelling, who or what can? The relatively new concept of "invented" spelling sounds bogus to many parents but has proved to be a useful phase in children's literacy development. The term "invented" is unfortunate because it suggests that children will and should be allowed to spell, or fail to spell, any way they want to. Foes of whole language accuse its adherents of negligently handing out "get out of spelling free" cards. But many mainstream educators, whether they favor youthful expression or phonics drills, see invention as a meaningful phase in children's earliest attempts to wrestle with the sounds and shapes of the alphabet. By late first grade, researchers say, many if not most children are managing to discern differences between consonants and vowels, and are eager to know if their efforts are "right." Once that happens, children can and will "invent" less as they begin to acquire more vocabulary and improve their ability to recognize word and sound patterns (but not necessarily rules) in ways that should promote more successful spelling.

Some traditionalist parents, teachers, and communities subscribe to a neo-Webster/McGuffey educational framework, and count George A. Thampy among their role models. A son of Christian émigrés from southern India, Thampy at age twelve became runner-up in the National Geographic Bee and winner of the Scripps National Spelling Bee in the same week in June, 2000. Home-schooled and religiously-schooled children have been disproportionally represented in the Bee and similar contests since the 1990s.

Others go further still. Since its inception during the Great Depression, FACE, the Foundation for American Christian Education, has been using Noah Webster's 1828 dictionary and publishing facsimile copies to spread the vocabulary, spelling, and moral values that are at the core of its trademarked" Noah Plan." Based in Virginia, FACE operates no schools itself but offers ideas and materials to like-minded educators and parents. "Two Dictionaries, Two Definitions: Which Dictionary is on Your Shelf?" the FACE web site asks. One example offers two definitions of *education*. Noah Webster's *American Dictionary of the English Language* tells us that "education comprehends... instruction and discipline intended to enlighten the understanding, correct the temper, and form the manners and habits of youth, and fit them for usefulness in their future stations. To give them religious education is indispensable" FACE finds Merriam-Webster's 1981 *New Collegiate Dictionary* inadequate for defining education as the "action or process of [developing mentally or morally]. It is interesting that an organization that presumably opposes the introduction of words minted after 1828 maintains a sophisticated presence on-line.

✏ ✏ ✏

How much does spelling still matter? For every dark prediction that spelling has withered in the face of texting, tweeting, instant messaging, or plain old inattention, there are many who believe spell-checkers and new educational strategies can be spelling's salvation. Now ubiquitous, these devices can be invaluable for preventing much orthographic embarrassment, but they are also a potentially insidious trap. Their implicit promise of spelling accuracy is beset by failures caused both by the devices and their users. Using spell-checkers correctly is faster, but not otherwise so different than that boring but time-honored advice to "look it up" in the dictionary: only someone who already has a really good idea of what she or he is looking for is likely to find it. Otherwise, opportunities for humiliation are legion. Automatic spell-checkers that now regularly pop up unbidden when someone tries to ask a question or make a comment on-line must be especially maddening for bad or simply careless or clumsy spellers. Spell-checkers embedded in writing programs are only as useful as the words and alternate choices the manufacturer has installed. Users, of course, are responsible for actually thinking and looking before they click. During my three years teaching college freshman, the word "aquatinted," a term only graphic artists are likely to use, showed up over and over. It turned out that "aquatinted" in the most popular spell-check program was the first alternate choice for the regularly misspelled but common word "acquainted." There are endless lists of the ten, fifty, hundred, etc. most misspelled English words. Virtually all of them include *millennium, minuscule, inoculate, harass, embarrassment, accommodate, occurrence, supersede, perseverance,* and *noticeable.* Each of those words was a deliberately misspelled answer to *Oops!,* a 2008 Sunday *Times* crossword. Avid puzzlers had to strain to figure out how to misspell all ten.

Over the years, many tools have purported to spare adults embarrassment and make spelling an educational game for children. The granddaddy of automated spelling instruction was Texas Instruments' 1978 Speak & Spell™, now a popular nostalgia item on eBay. It has spawned many imitators. A 1996 computer program called "English Sound-Spel" had a rather different agenda. This brainchild of the American Literacy Council, a spelling reform group, has roots that go back to the 1876 International Convention for the Amendment of English Orthography. Although it could function as a standard spell-checker, Sound-Spel's avowed mission is to use a computer program to automatically "translate" texts into the Literacy Council's version of reformed spelling. A key developer and promoter was Edward Rondthaler, the spelling reformer who died at age 104 in 2009.

Other electronic spelling aids have more modest expectations. Franklin Electronic Publishers of New Jersey, which has links to the Scripps Bee, has since 1986 produced "language learning solutions" that the company says are used in twenty thousand classrooms. Many of their products are oriented to travelers, college students, and non-English speakers. One early Franklin product, the Webster's Spelling Corrector, priced at $25, was apparently offered for sale soon after Vice President Dan Quayle's famous 1982 gaffe. Said the ad copy, "Can it really be... potatoe? Certainly not, as you'll learn from Franklin's 80,000-word spelling corrector." The emergence of both "talking" and silent electronic language devices, along with magnifiers and other accessibility products have also been a boon for persons with disabilities.

Faster, easier, and cheaper than the telegram at its peak, texting and its sidekicks are usually informal condensed messages that have prompted teens and others to write more often, creating some new protocols for grammar and spelling, even as many tweets and instant messages seem to be, and often are, chaotic and trivial. As these new texts have begun to trickle into classrooms, teachers and linguists have reacted with both horror and hope. In a 2002 article titled, "Nu Shortcuts in School R 2 Much 4 Teachers" reporter Jennifer 8. Lee

(Yes, 8, not 'eight' is her middle name) found educators spanning the pedagogical gamut. One teacher observed that text argot is not necessarily more efficient than standard spelling. "I understand 'cuz,'" she said, "but what's with 'wuz'? It's the same amount [sic] of letters as 'was' so what's the point." Others saw it as a way to unleash creativity and get students writing before making the transition to more standard forms. It seems likely that these optimists are whole language devotees.

Commentators at Language Log, a well-regarded website housed at the University of Pennsylvania since 2003, have been mostly bullish on texting as part of a proliferating language universe. When Ben Zimmer brought up texting concerns at Language Log in 2008, the consensus was that neither the English language nor its spelling was under serious attack. Quoting linguist David Crystal, who came to texting's defense in his book, *Txtng: the gr8 db8*, Zimmer asserted that text messages do not cause bad spelling because "you have to know how to spell before you can text." In an article titled, "Linguistic Ruin? LOL! Instant Messaging and Teen Language," two University of Toronto linguists extensively studied seventy-two teens' instant messages and declared this new form of communication to be vibrant, dynamic, and not a threat to English as we know it. "Will electronically mediated language...lead to shortcuts in spelling and the elimination of spaces between words..." asked William Safire nine months before his death at age seventy-nine. "Of course it will. Should educators resist the trend in the name of thoughtfulness and clarity? Sometimes, not always." .

There is much evidence that texters can be as snobbish about correct parlance as many prescriptivists of yore. Crystal's book included a nine-page appendix of accepted number and letter combinations. Mocking the spelling of rushed and random "tweets" seems to have become an electronic game of "gotcha." Among many other casual or spelling-challenged celebrity tweeters, actor John Cusack has caught flak from better-educated or just more particular followers. Republican Sen. Charles Grassley of Iowa, a seventy-six year old newcomer to twitterdom, was once savaged by a columnist not only for his ideology but for misspelling "intelligent" minus the second "l."

Nor is this just an on-line phenomenon. In 2008, two Dartmouth graduates armed with Wite-Out™ and marking pens terrorized or at least annoyed shopkeepers and public agencies from Boston to Seattle, New Orleans to Atlanta during a three-month crusade. Jeff Deck and Benjamin Herson focused on eliminating misplaced apostrophes, but also tried to leave no misspellings behind. On Chicago's Milwaukee Avenue, a furniture store had botched both "Milwaukee" by transposing the "a" and "u," while inside the store had added an extra "n" in "dining room." The finicky young men could not persuade the shopkeeper to fix these glaring errors. Occasionally, good spellers will consider the self-esteem of the spelling-challenged. The *Washington Post*'s "Miss Manners" in 2008 advised an editor and proofreader to be kind when s/he visited a drugstore filled with signs that were professionally printed but peppered with misspellings. We cannot, said the etiquette authority, "run around insulting people, which is what an amazing number of people do when they detect errors..." Instead, she advised bringing spelling lapses to the attention of the offending business's front office. Meanwhile, Randy Cohen, formerly the *New York Times* Sunday ethicist, was not ready to approve hiring just any spelling and grammar challenged individual who applied, but suggested help for those whose only deficit was poor English.

Strategic misspelling is regularly used in commercial undertakings where there is a premium on unique product names that can be trademarked. The trick is to spell these in ways that honor, if not strictly obey, the conventions of spelling to the extent that the company or product name seems clever and memorable, not just misspelled. Acclaimed orthographer Richard L. Venezkey, writing in 1999, defined four varieties of these oddly spelled names. The first consist of words that obey spelling rules; names such as *Tylenol* or the *Beatles*. More marginal are run-ons or aggressive contractions. He offered *Mixit* and *Read 'Em and Reap*. A third category introduces "clear violations" of spelling practice, including mash-ups such as

Exxon and *Shu-Wite*. Finally, he took an early interest in computer-influenced spellings like *2night* (or *nite*) that crossbreed letters with numbers and other symbols.

Venezky's careful analysis has real-world consequences especially in the on-line environment. In recent years, both deliberate and accidental misspellings of Internet domain names have meant frustration for many and profits for some businesses that take advantage of unintended "clicks" by bad or careless spellers. Similarly, on-line auctions can be a snake pit for inattentive spellers. At sites such as eBay, savvy consumers who deliberately look for misspelled items can often buy them for a pittance, thanks to minimal bidding competition. Spammers and other on-line purveyors of fake or illegal products have used deliberate misspellings and quirky characters to avoid filters. One favorite ploy: "vi@gra."

But these are not necessarily language flaws that need to be fixed. As Venezky and other have pointed out, English has become a global success, the go-to language, due in part to its playfulness and leniency that also acknowledge its complicated ancestry. The future is likely to be even more complex. English repays attentive spellers with puns and other clever usages, made possible by its maddening spelling. Rich in homonyms and homophones, English, according to Venezky, fosters creativity. He cited a bakery called "All You Knead." This does not work so well in Finnish or Turkish, he observed. Conversely, simplified spelling schemes have historically tended to produce language that has been simplified into a bewildering mishmash, stripping words of their singularity and potential.

The spelling of given names is another kind of problem, likely to give rise to fanciful constructions that defy orthography in the name of individuality and may condemn unlucky children to a lifetime of daily aggravation. Hard to spell surnames, on the other hand, often result from efforts to transliterate family names from languages other than English. In 2010, Alaska Senator Lisa Murkowski waged a successful write-in battle that hinged on her ability to teach enough supporters to actually write in her name on the ballot. Her opponent, a man named Miller, challenged the inevitable misspellings, including one perpetrated early on by her own election team, but Murkowski prevailed. "In Alaska Voters' Spelling Bee, She's the Queen," said a headline announcing her political triumph.

Some obviously foreign words imported into English face competing spellings. One example is the Hebrew word for the eight-day winter festival of lights that is usually rendered as "Chanukah" or "Hanukkah." Microsoft's spell-checker allows either. The late leader of Libya accrued a variety of spellings, among them "Gaddafi," preferred by most news services including the English service of Al-Jazzera, while the White House has favored "Qaddafi". Merriam-Webster on-line suggests "Gadhafi" or alternatively "Qaddafi".

A popular "adult" version of invented spelling shows up as an electronic chain letter from time to time, prefaced by the come-on, "believe it or not, you can read this." A brief excerpt will suffice: "Amzanig huh? Yaeh, and I awlyas thought slpeling was ipmorantt." The trick here, attributed to Cambridge University researchers, is that if the first and last letter of each word is in the right place, the brain presumably does the rest. Tellingly, the word "thought" is spelled normally: the first letter/last letter formula is too ambiguous to accommodate this ugly "ugh" word.

Few traces of Teddy Roosevelt, Andrew Carnegie, and Brander Matthews' spelling reform scheme have survived in official Washington. In April 2008, U.S. public printer Robert C. Tapella of the Government Printing Office unveiled the thirtieth edition of an official government style manual, first published in 1894, but offered not a whisper of the events of 1906. The manual which included a fifteen-page spelling section based on *Webster's Third New International Dictionary*, is austere, focusing mainly on easily-confused homonyms and homophones. It cautions users to tread carefully when using spell-checkers, saying, "The tendency of some producers of computer-assisted publications to rely on the limited capability of some spell-checking programs adds importance to this list."

The GPO has remained adamantly attached to the -*ugh*, so

detested by generations of spelling reformers and efficiency experts. Such *ugh* words as *enough* or *through* are now so unexceptionable that these words no longer even show up on the newest list. More puzzling are the *-ogue* words. *Catalog*, minus the *-ue* was a 1906 success story and is still preferred to this day, as is *cataloger*. Yet GPO orthographers still insist on *dialogue, epilogue, demagogue, homologue, travelogue, pedagogue, prologue, monologue,* and *Decalogue*. Some of today's dictionaries allow or even prefer the simpler *-log* ending, but not the United States' printer.

"I'll have the misspelled 'Ceasar' salad and the improperly hyphenated veal osso-buco."

"Hail, Ceasar"

In 1928, nine years after Theodore Roosevelt died at the age of sixty, Charles Scribner's Sons published TR's boyhood diaries. He had begun them at age nine as his family embarked on a year-long Grand Tour of Europe that commenced in August 1868. *Theodore Roosevelt's Diaries of Boyhood and Youth* revealed his bold, if messy, penmanship, and a vocabulary and curiosity that many a college student then or now should envy.

Spelling was quite another matter. Said the diaries' anonymous editor, "The spelling has been retained as Young Theodore wrote it." In his first entry of "August 10th Munday," Teedie, as his family called their second child, continued, "I had an attack of the *Asmer...* The first fig [from the family's garden] was *eatten* that evening." The next day, bound for a year in Europe, he wrote "It was *verry* hard parting from our friends."

Indeed, parting with *verry* and some other doubled consonants including *t*, as in *citty* seemed to be especially difficult for this aspiring journaler. By June 4, 1869, Teedie was reliably spelling *asthma*, the ailment that dogged his childhood and impaired his health. But *verry* remained very much in play. Leaving England on July 13, he called the Thames "a verry, verry small river or a large creek." On November 15, 1869, the young traveler mentioned that "I wrote a letter to Eideth," his New York neighbor and playmate. Most likely, he had learned to spell her name by the time Edith Kermit Carow became his second wife in 1886.

Back in New York at last in 1870, Teedie's spelling actually seemed to decline, possibly because his parents were less likely to be reading their son's journals. In June and July, young Roosevelt "stayed in the Citty," complained of a "swoolen" gland, noted a "Rainey" day, "built a firre," and "bout a fishing aparratus."

By the time Teedie, nearing thirteen, resumed his journals in August 1871, most but not all of his spelling glitches had vanished. As the 1928 editor noted, "The reader will observe that the author's spelling has improved."

Indeed it had. "Teedie" became TR, moving from strength

to strength as an accomplished writer, naturalist, hunter, soldier, politician, and president of the United States. He could have ignored the spelling reformers, but the youth who had struggled "verry" hard to tame his spelling was willing in 1906 to take on Congress, the newspapers, and haughty prescriptivists in what turned out to be one of his rare defeats.

Like TR, and Noah Webster, for that matter, we remain somewhere between orthographic hell and spelling Nirvana. Our spelling, even as it mutates and continues to admit words from all over, will likely remain as rich in annoyance as it is in achievement and history. So, how DO you spell "Roosevelt"? Come on. Of course you can spell it. Sound it out. It's just spelling!